Visual Science Encyclopedia

Water

▲ Oxbows on the Green River, Utah. These water-eroded canyons were created over millions of years as the river cut into the Colorado plateau.

How to use this book

Every word defined in this book can be found in alphabetical order on pages 3 to 47. There is also a full index on page 48. A number of other features will help you get the most out of the *Visual Science Encyclopedia*. They are shown below.

Here you will find the first word defined on any left-hand page.

Each word is shown in bold so it is easy to find.

Other words defined in the book are highlighted in bold.

Plus, many entries point to related words of interest.

Here you will find the last word defined on any right-hand page.

Each new letter of the alphabet is clearly marked to help you find the word you are looking for quicker.

Illustrations for some words complement the text and provide further information on a topic.

First published in 2002 by Atlantic Europe Publishing Company Ltd

Author
Brian Knapp, BSc, PhD

Art Director
Duncan McCrae, BSc

Senior Designer
Adele Humphries, BA, PGCE

Editors
Lisa Magloff, BA, and
Mary Sanders, BSc

Illustrations
David Woodroffe

Designed and produced by
EARTHSCAPE EDITIONS

Reproduced in Malaysia by
Global Colour

Printed in Hong Kong by
Wing King Tong Company Ltd.

Visual Science Encyclopedia
Volume 6 *Water*
A CIP record for this book is available from the British Library

ISBN 1-86214-024-3

Picture credits
All photographs are from the Earthscape Editions photolibrary.

This product is manufactured from sustainable managed forests. For every tree cut down, at least one more is planted.

A

Abrasion

The wearing away of rock by moving **water** that carries small rock particles. The large pieces are slowly worn away and fine powder is produced.

The effect is much the same as using sandpaper. **Rivers** carry fine rock particles (**sediment**) that abrade the banks and bed of the **river channel**. At the same time, the rock particles bump together, making them finer and more rounded. This is called **attrition**.

Alluvial fan

A broad cone of material that builds up in mountainous areas where a fast-flowing **river** enters a flatter valley. Because the speed of the **water** slows as it reaches the valley, the coarser and heavier material is dropped, and it gradually builds up into a fan-shaped cone. (*See also:* **Alluvium**.)

Alluvium

Any material laid down by a **river**. The smaller pieces are also often called **silt** or mud. The larger pieces are called pebbles, cobbles and **boulders**.

Alluvium is laid down on the bed of a river and also across the surrounding land when a river **floods** over its banks. The material it is carrying then settles out and creates a layer. This layer is often silty or muddy and that is why people use the words 'silt' or 'mud' instead of alluvium. However, the alluvium that spreads over a **flood plain** may also contain **sand** and even pebbles.

You can see alluvium by looking at the banks of a river. They are made not only of rock, but of alluvium. (*See also:* **Sediment**.)

▲ **Alluvium** – Running water can carry a wide variety of materials from boulders and pebbles to grit, sand and silt, and finally to clay. These pictures show silt and clay in the Colorado River. The silt settles out, but the clay remains in suspension.

▲ **Alluvium** – Pebbles, grit and sand.

Aqueduct

A **canal**, tunnel, or pipe designed to carry **water**. Aqueducts have been in use since ancient times. Some of the largest modern aqueducts are in California, where there is a great need to supply **irrigation** water to farmers and **drinking water** to cities such as Los Angeles. The California Aqueduct, for example, is over 700km long.

◀▼ **Aqueduct** – Aqueducts are essential for carrying water from places of surplus to places of demand. In the past stone aqueducts were often used, as shown in the picture on the left from France. Modern high-capacity aqueducts (as shown by the California Aqueduct in the lower picture) are concrete-lined channels.

Aquiclude

A rock layer that does not allow **water** to flow through it. Rocks that form aquicludes include granite, **clay** and shale.

Because most rocks are, in fact, aquicludes, the word is not commonly used. Instead, people use the word **aquifer** to describe the less common kind of rocks that allow water to flow through them.

Springs often occur at the junction of an aquifer and an aquiclude. The springs appear at the top of the aquiclude and at the bottom of the aquifer.

Aquifer

A water-bearing rock. Chalk, limestone and sandstone are typical water-bearing rocks. If a large part of an aquifer is trapped between two layers of watertight rocks (**aquicludes**), the trapped **water** is called **artesian water**. Aquifers are vital sources of **drinking water** in most countries of the world. However, they can be overused if the amount taken out is greater than the amount added by **rainfall**. The water in the rock helps keep the rock from becoming compacted, so when too much water is removed from the aquifer, through water 'mining', the land often collapses. The land surface in the San Joaquin Valley in California has sunk several metres as a result of

water mining. Once the rock has compacted, it will never expand again, so the amount of water that can be stored is reduced. (*See also:* **Ground water**; **Spring**; **Well**.)

Artesian water

Ground water that comes from an **aquifer** trapped between two confining watertight beds (**aquicludes**). The **water** may seep into an aquifer where the rock is exposed in hills; but because it is confined between watertight layers, it has no means of escape. As a result, the water in the artesian aquifer is often under considerable pressure.

When a **well** is drilled to an artesian aquifer, the water often gushes out onto the surface,

sometimes with enough force to make a fountain. For example, for a long time the fountains in London's Trafalgar Square were run using the natural pressure of the artesian aquifer below London rather than with pumps.

Artesian pressure is reduced over time as the water flows to the surface. As a result, bore holes that begin flowing without assistance often have to be pumped after a few years. The world's largest artesian **basin** lies under much of northern central Australia. One of the largest artesian basins in the United States is the Olgallala aquifer, which lies to the east of the Rocky Mountains, under much of the Great Plains.

Attrition

The wearing away of particles of rock as they bounce together in moving **water**.

Attrition is partly responsible for the rounded shape of **river**-borne material and for the way in which pebbles become reduced in size to make **sand** grains. (*See also:* **Abrasion**.)

B

Badlands

A pattern of gullies in a landscape of soft rocks where there is no plant cover to hold the soil in place.

Badlands are a feature of **river basins** in semi-arid parts of the world. Badlands National Park in South Dakota shows these features clearly. However, overfarming has also produced badlands in places where they would not naturally occur.

Barrage

A large barrier across a **river**, intended to control the flow of **water**. Contrast it to a weir, which is a barrier across a small river.

A barrage is made out of concrete and has steel gates. The gates are lowered or raised to allow more or less water to flow through

▲ **Barrage** – A barrage on the Mississippi River.

them. The height of the gates is constantly adjusted to keep the water level above the barrage deep enough for boats to navigate, but low enough to allow the river to flow as naturally as possible without **flooding** the valley above the barrage. (*See also:* **Dam**; **Hydroelectric power**; **Water power**.)

▼ **Aquifer/Artesian water** – If an aquifer is trapped between two aquicludes, the water filling up the aquifer comes under pressure. It is artesian water. It can be released by drilling wells. This makes a water supply that, at least to begin with, does not require pumps to bring it to the surface.

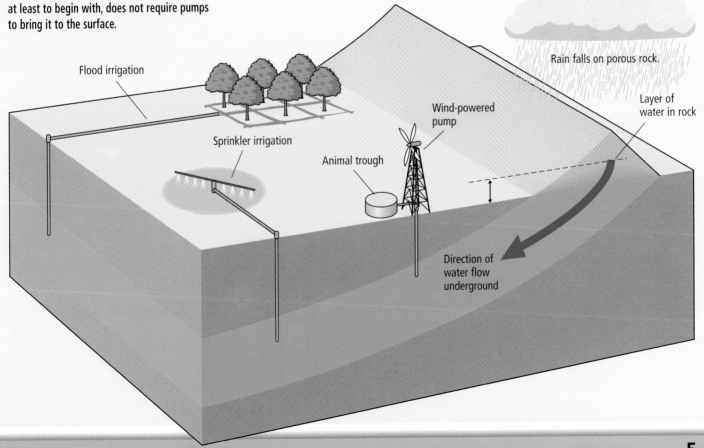

Flood irrigation

Sprinkler irrigation

Animal trough

Wind-powered pump

Rain falls on porous rock.

Layer of water in rock

Direction of water flow underground

Basin, river basin

The area drained by a **river** and its **tributaries**. It is also called a **drainage basin**.

The boundary of a river basin is called a **watershed** or divide. The **river channels** in a basin normally occupy less than 5% of the land, and even in times of **flood** it is rare for surface **water** to cover more than one-fifth of the basin.

The river network consists of **head waters**, or **branches**, which form at the edge of the drainage basin, then join together to make a master, or trunk, stream.

Billabong

A name used in Australia for any seasonal pond, including **oxbow lakes**.

Bog

A region of waterlogged land. The name bog is usually reserved for waterlogged uplands in cool regions such as Scotland and Ireland. It is a form of **wetland**.

Boiling point of water

The temperature at which **water** turns into **steam**, or water **vapour**. At sea level water boils at 100°C. The boiling point varies with

▲ **Bog** – Rannock Moor in the Highlands of Scotland.

altitude: it is slightly higher than 100°C at low altitudes where the air pressure is high and slightly lower than 100°C at high altitudes, where the air pressure is low.

For example, air pressure is lower high up on a mountain than on a lowland plain, and high up on a mountain the boiling point of **water** can be several degrees below 100°C. This explains why hot drinks made with boiling water never taste truly hot when made on mountains, and also why food takes a long time to cook at high altitude or may never cook properly at all.

▶ **Boiling point of water** – Boiling is indicated by internal evaporation. We see it when water vapour forms inside the liquid water and gathers together to form bubbles before bursting to the surface.

Bore

A wave of **water** that is forced upstream in some **rivers** at the onset of a rising **tide** or **flood** tide. Bores are only found in cone-shaped **estuaries** where the rising tide raises the level of water in the estuary above that of the river and forces the river to flow back on itself.

Boulder

A large fragment of rock that is hardly ever moved by a **river**. Boulders are more than 256mm across, while cobbles and pebbles are smaller than this. Many boulders cannot be moved except by the largest **flood**. (*See also:* **Sediment**.)

Brackish water

Water that contains more than 1g of **dissolved** salts per litre, but which is less salty than the sea, which has 35g of dissolved salts per litre.

Braided river

A **river** with a pattern of natural channels cut in **sand**, gravel and pebbles that intertwine across a broad area in the centre of a valley.

It is one of the two types of patterns of **river channel**, the other

▲ **Braided river** – A braided river is readily identified by its multitude of channels.

being meandering (*see:* **Meander**).

Braided channels are known for their shifting islands. Because the material is coarse, it does not stick together like **clay** and so cannot form a high bank to a channel. As a result, braided channels cannot have steep sides, and to compensate for this, a braided river channel has to be much wider than a meandering river carrying the same amount of **water**. However, braided rivers can be easier to **ford** than meandering rivers, a feature appreciated in the past by pioneers such as those on America's 19th-century Oregon Trail. The Platte River is a typically braided river and was described by one pioneer as 'A mile wide and an inch deep'.

Branch

A **tributary** close to a **watershed** that is regarded as being the starting point of a **river** system. An alternative term for branch is **fork**.

▶ **Bridging point of a river** – The oldest bridge in Bath spans the River Avon, England. This bridge was designed to have shops on it, and some still remain. This illustrates the importance of bridges as a way of bringing people together. When a bridge connects two communities, there is a new opportunity for trade, and the shops were built to take advantage of this opportunity.

Bridging point of a river

The name given to a place that develops where a bridge is built across a **river** or **estuary**. The bridge makes land routes converge and gives more opportunity for trade by people living at the bridging point.

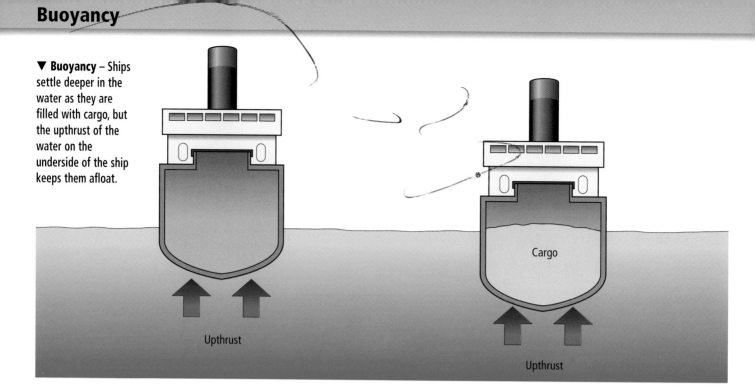

▼ **Buoyancy** – Ships settle deeper in the water as they are filled with cargo, but the upthrust of the water on the underside of the ship keeps them afloat.

Upthrust

Cargo

Upthrust

Buoyancy

The property of floating, first explained by the Ancient Greek mathematician Archimedes. Anything that is completely or partially submerged in **water** is supported by an upwards, or buoyant, force called upthrust. The size of this force equals the weight of the water that is moved aside by the floating body. Thus a boat placed in a **river** will settle until the weight of the river water it pushes aside is equal to its own weight. If more weight is placed in the boat and it becomes heavier, it will settle lower in the water.

C

Canal

An artificial waterway designed to be used for transportation.

The major canals of the world include: Suez Canal (opened 1869) 170km long, 150m wide and 13m deep; Panama Canal (opened 1914) 85km long, 81m wide and 11m deep; St. Lawrence Seaway 3,800km (includes Welland Canal 45km); Keil Canal (opened 1914) 100km long; Rhine Danube Canal (completion 1996); Corinth Canal (opened 1893) 6km gorge over 80m deep.

The first ancient large canal system was built by the Chinese in the 3rd century BC. By the 7th century AD the system had become the Grand Canal that connected the Yangtze River to Beijing, a distance of about 1,600km. It remains the longest artificial waterway in the world.

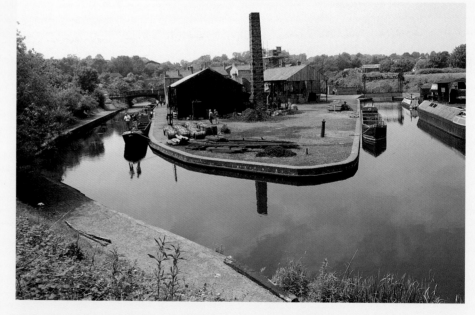

▲ **Canal** – Canals were important in helping industrialisation in both North America and Europe. Many now lie disused because industries no longer depend on water in the way they once did.

The Romans built many canals in Europe. But the main development of European and American canals was in the 18th

and 19th centuries. The canals were of major importance in the Industrial Revolution. They all included a **lock**, invented in the Netherlands in about 1373 and used on all canals ever since. The lock allowed boats to be raised or lowered around a weir or **barrage**.

Canals were very important in America in opening up the country. By the end of the 19th century there were 6,500km of canals in America. They were very important in linking the Great Lakes to navigable **rivers** such as the Mississippi.

Canal building slowed with the introduction of the railways, and many early canals have now been abandoned.

An artificial waterway designed to carry **water** for **drinking**, **irrigation** and so on is called an **aqueduct**.

Canyon

A steep-sided valley, usually in a desert or near-desert area. The world's largest canyon is the Grand Canyon in Arizona, which is 360km long, 1.6km deep and up to 50km wide.

Cataract

Another name for a series of **rapids** or a cascading series of **waterfalls** on a large **river**. The Nile in Egypt and the Paraña in South America both have cataracts.

Chemical weathering

The way that **water** and natural acids in the environment react with rock to turn the solid rock into soil.

◄ **Chemical weathering** – In this experiment two blocks of chalk are placed in a beaker. Vinegar is added. The chalk fizzes and begins to dissolve, passing into solution. This is a fast version of the chemical weathering that occurs in nature, where the dissolved rock can then be carried away even by slow-flowing rivers.

Clay, mud

The smallest size of material (**sediment**). A clay particle is smaller than 1 micron (a thousandth of a millimetre) across. Clay in a **river** bed is often called mud. It is the material that colours the **water** during times of high flow and **flood**. Mud is left behind after a flood, coating the floors and walls of flooded buildings.

Clay and mud are also the most fertile part of the material carried by a river, so that when they are deposited over a **flood plain** during a flood, they bring natural fertility to the land.

In the past people relied on the fertile clay brought by floods. The Nile flood is the most famous example. Every year the river flooded the lower Nile River Valley in Egypt and brought both water and fertiliser. When the flood waters went down, the farmers grew their crops on the layer of clay deposited by it. For thousands of years this flood enabled farmers to grow enough food for all of Egypt to eat. However, since the building of the Aswan High Dam, the flood no longer occurs and so the lower Nile no longer receives its annual supply of clay.

Clean water

Water that is free from **disease-carrying organisms**, such as bacteria and viruses, harmful chemicals and particles of dirt.

It requires enormous effort to clean water to a standard that is suitable for **drinking**. It is relatively easy to make water look clean. Pieces of dirt can be removed by letting water stand still for a while so that they settle out. Small particles can be made to clump together by adding a special chemical, often aluminium sulphate. After this, the water is passed through a filter made from a bed of **sand**.

But although the water that comes through this process may look clean, it is not biologically or chemically clean.

Getting water chemically clean is very difficult because water is the world's most common **solvent**. This means that water can **dissolve** a large number of substances. Gases dissolve in water while it is in the air and fertilisers and other chemicals dissolve in it as it passes through soils and along **river channels**.

As water stays in contact with the ground longer, more minerals will dissolve in it. That is why water pumped from underground often has a very high amount of dissolved minerals (hence the name mineral water).

To remove these minerals, the water is treated with chemicals that cause the dissolved materials to settle out (precipitate).

It takes much more complicated treatment to remove industrial pollutants such as metals and oil.

Many disease-carrying micro-organisms live in water. Some of them can be killed by passing the water through a tank containing beneficial bacteria and by adding a disinfectant to the water, usually in the form of chlorine. (*Compare with:* **Polluted water**.)

(*See also:* **Water supply** and **Well**.)

◀▲ **Clean water** – An engineer (left) examines a sample of polluted water (above) before it is treated.

Cliff, river cliff

Any very steep slope formed by natural processes. Cliffs are too steep for soil and are always bare rock.

Cliffs can be created by **rivers** as they undercut their banks. These cliffs, called river cliffs, are on the outside of the curving section (**meander**) of a river and may be between a few metres and hundreds of metres high.

Condensation

Water **vapour** condenses into liquid **water** when the temperature of the air falls. One way in which air cools is when it comes into contact with a cold surface. That is why, for example, a glass containing **ice** cubes soon gathers a coating of condensation. Warm air flowing over a cold ocean has the same effect; in this case contact with condensation takes place through the cooler air and results in fog.

Air can also cool if it rises in the atmosphere. That is the reason why clouds form. In this case condensation forms on tiny dust

▲ **Confluence** – This is Pittsburgh, where the Allegheny and the Monongahela Rivers meet at the Golden Triangle, close to the city centre. You can see the location of the original fort (the white lines just behind the fountain) close to the confluence, showing the strategic advantage of a confluence site.

and salt particles suspended in the air. If the air is very cold, then water vapour changes directly into **ice crystals**. This is called **sublimation**.

Confluence

A place where two **rivers** meet.

Confluences have often been the site of important towns and cities because of their good natural route advantages. Cities built on confluences include Pittsburgh (a confluence of two **tributaries** of the Ohio River) and Koblenz (confluence of the Rhine and Mosel, Germany).

Continental divide

The line that separates areas of land that drain into one **ocean** from areas draining into another ocean.

Crater lake

A **lake** that fills the top of a volcano.

Crater lakes form when a volcano explodes so violently that it leaves the magma chamber below it empty. At the same time, the enormous explosion causes many earthquakes in the rocks above, and they begin to crack and weaken. The top of the volcano then collapses down into the magma chamber, leaving a huge circular pit known as a caldera.

In time, the caldera fills with **water** to make a crater lake.

▼ **Condensation** – Condensation on the inside of a cold window-pane in a warm kitchen.

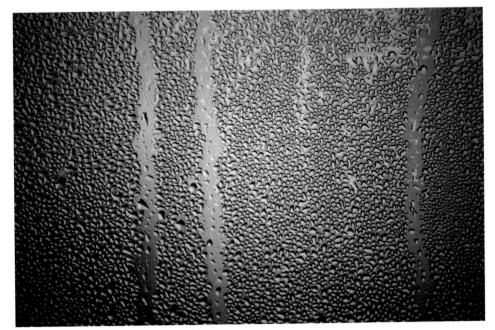

Crevasse

A deep crack in the surface of a moving mass of **ice**, either an ice sheet or a **glacier**. A crevasse forms because the ice near the surface is brittle, while the deeper ice is under much more pressure and acts more like a liquid. As the deeper ice flows, it begins to drag the surface ice along. If the ice flows down an even slope, then no crevasses occur. But if the ice flows over a rock step or around a bend, the deep ice is able to flow over these obstructions, while the ice at the surface is too brittle to flow and breaks up into crevasses. As a result, the pattern of crevasses on the surface of ice gives good clues to how the deeper ice is moving. (*See also:* **Ice crystals**.)

D

Dam

An artificial wall or embankment designed to hold back **water**. The water held back makes a **reservoir** (sometimes called a '**lake**' if it is large).

Earth and rock dams are broad structures with gently sloping sides and a very wide base. They are used only for dams of modest height. An earth dam is usually faced with stone so that it is not eroded by running water or lake waves. Masonry and concrete are used to build the world's tallest dams, or where a dam must be strong enough to block a narrow valley. The world's biggest dam will be the Three Gorges dam on the Yangtze River in China. It is currently under construction and due to be completed in 2009.

Dams are important because they often do several useful things. For example, they hold back **river** water to prevent **floods**;

▲▼ **Dam** – The Glen Canyon dam on the Colorado River, Arizona. The diagram below shows how water is led over the dam to the turbine house at its foot. This generates electricity.

they also store water in reservoirs for use in **irrigation**, to produce **hydroelectric power**, or to keep rivers flowing in times of **drought**. Reservoirs can also be used for recreation.

The construction of dams and reservoirs is of concern to environmentalists because it often destroys the natural environment. (*See also:* **Barrage**.)

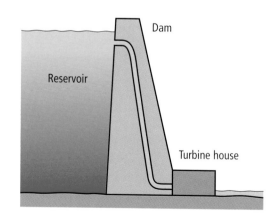

Dehydration

The excessive loss of **water** from the body.

The human body is over 90% water. The body loses water all the time – about 1.2 litres a day – and the water must be replaced. Normal water loss is replaced by drinking, and we do not give any thought to it. The body regulates the rate of replacement by making us feel thirsty. However, there are certain circumstances in which we do not replace what we lose, and that results in a serious illness called dehydration.

Our bodies may lose excessive water by sweating, for example, in a long race, or because we have gone through a long period without drinking such as in disasters when **water supplies** fail. Dehydration may be caused by an illness such as dysentery in which body fluids are rapidly lost.

Dehydration tends to cause a slow loss of body weight – about a kilogramme a day. Once someone has lost about 13 litres of water, sweating stops, and so the body loses its ability to get rid of excess heat. As a result, the body temperature rises dramatically. Death from dehydration is therefore usually not by direct loss in body weight, but often by shock and heart failure due to a rise in body temperature.

The way to treat dehydration is not simply with water, but with a salt and water mixture. If it is given gradually, the body will then begin to recover.

Delta

A fan-shaped area of **sediment** built up at the mouth of a **river**.

The world's biggest deltas include: Nile Delta, Egypt; Mississippi Delta; Ganges/ Brahmaputra Delta, Bangladesh; Mekong Delta, Vietnam; Yellow River Delta, China.

(*See also:* **Drainage**.)

▼ **Delta** – This side view of a delta shows that it builds forwards.

Desalinisation

The removal of salt from **sea water**. Areas with few natural **rivers**, such as deserts and islands, use desalinisation systems. Desalinisation is used in the Caribbean as well as in desert areas such as the Middle East.

Desalinisation can be achieved by heating salt water until it boils. The **vaporised** water is then cooled and the **condensed** water is collected. This is very costly in terms of energy and is only suited to countries that have large reserves of cheap fuel.

An alternative process uses thin sheets of plastic, called membranes, that allow **water** to pass through them but keep the salt out. This process is not suited to sea water but works well with **fresh water** that has a high mineral content or when the water is slightly salty ('**brackish**'). This process is called reverse osmosis.

It is also possible to remove salt from water by **freezing** (*see:* **Ice crystals**). In areas where freezing temperatures do not naturally occur, this process also requires energy.

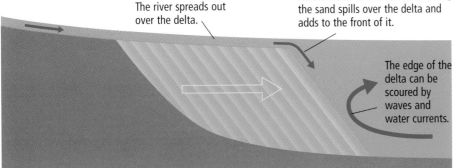

The river spreads out over the delta.

As the water enters the lake or sea, the sand spills over the delta and adds to the front of it.

The edge of the delta can be scoured by waves and water currents.

Nile Delta

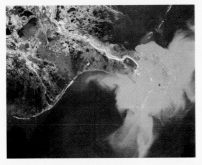

Mississippi Delta

Bird's foot delta

◄► **Delta** – Deltas can be categorised into fan or bird-foot shapes.

Fan-shaped

Dike

A long embankment, often looking like a natural **levee**, that is used to prevent **river water** from **flooding** low-lying land.

A dike is usually made with a core of soil and faced with stone or rush mats to prevent **erosion**. The top is broad and is often planted with grass to help stabilise it. In the United States artificial dikes or artificially heightened dikes are also called levees. (*See also:* **Groyne**.)

▲ **Dike** – The Embankment in London is a stone dike. The front is a wall that has recently been raised to prevent flooding. Notice how the seats have had to be placed on raised platforms so that people can see over the wall while seated.

Diseases

Water-borne diseases are an important worldwide problem. Almost 250 million people each year contract a water-borne disease, and about 10 million of them die from such diseases.

One of the most serious of these diseases is cholera. Today, cholera affects tropical countries in particular, but is certainly not confined to them. The connection between cholera and the contamination of **drinking water** by raw sewage was first recognised in London in 1854. This led directly to rapid attempts by industrialised countries to purify their **water**. There may be more than a million people suffering from cholera today. It is a disease that particularly affects the slum areas of developing world cities where sanitation is poor.

Bilharzia, or schistosomiasis, is another water-borne disease that affects 200 million people. It relies on host snails in the water. Unfortunately, the still waters that the snails live in are being extended with the construction of more and more **reservoirs** and **irrigation** channels. All bodies of water in Africa are now contaminated with the snail, including all of the Great Rift Valley **lakes**.

Legionnaire's disease is another disease connected with water. It grows in the water used in air-conditioning systems that are not sufficiently clean. It is resistant to the chemical chlorine – normally regarded as a sure way of purifying water. However, Legionnaire's disease does not affect drinking water.

Malaria is one of the world's biggest killer diseases. It is carried by the anopheles mosquito. Two

▼ **Diseases** – This little girl is washing the family cooking pot in a disease-carrying sewer. Although many slum dwellers are aware of the risks of using polluted water sources such as this, they often provide the only water supply.

billion people are at permanent risk from malaria, with about 130 million cases reported each year, mainly in Africa and Asia. Malaria is responsible for one-third of all infant deaths. The larval stages of the mosquito develop in stagnant water.

Onchocerciasis, also called river blindness, is a disease of tropical countries produced by the bite of the black fly, which breeds on rivers.

(*See also:* **Dehydration**.)

Dissolve

To cause one substance to disperse into another so that it seems to disappear. **Water** is the world's most common **solvent** and a wide range of substances dissolve in it.

Salt, carbon dioxide and oxygen gases dissolve in water. All three are found in **sea water**. Carbon dioxide is also dissolved in water under pressure to make fizzy (carbonated) drinks.

Gases in the air readily dissolve in water. Often this is a good thing, such as when oxygen dissolves in water to provide the oxygen necessary to marine life. But it can also be a danger, such as when pollution gases like sulphur and nitrogen oxide dissolve in **raindrops** and then fall as acid rain.

When acid gases are dissolved in water, they can react with rocks and rot them away. Limestone rocks dissolve in water containing carbon dioxide. Over time such solutions widen cracks in limestone, allowing them to form tunnels and caves.

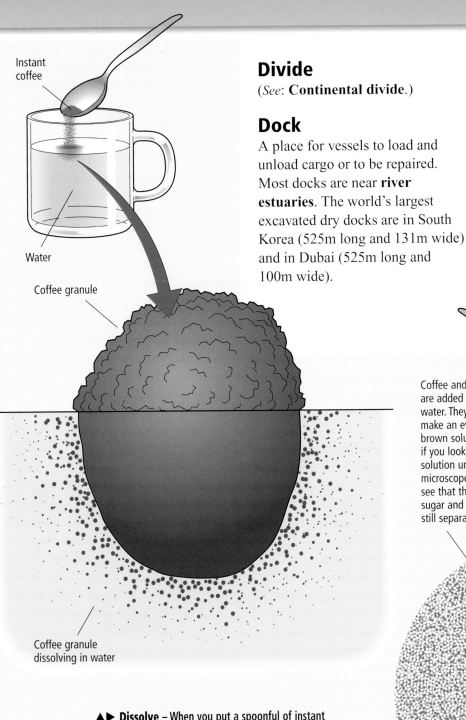

Instant coffee

Water

Coffee granule

Coffee granule dissolving in water

Divide
(*See*: **Continental divide**.)

Dock
A place for vessels to load and unload cargo or to be repaired. Most docks are near **river estuaries**. The world's largest excavated dry docks are in South Korea (525m long and 131m wide) and in Dubai (525m long and 100m wide).

Drainage
The removal of unwanted **water** from land surfaces. Drainage is used in towns and cities to get rid of **rain water** and on farmland to prevent or reduce waterlogging of flat **clay** land. Drainage of **river deltas** is often called reclamation. (*See also:* **Runoff**.)

Drainage basin
The total area that drains to a **river** or a **lake**. Another related term is **watershed**. (*See also:* **Basin**.)

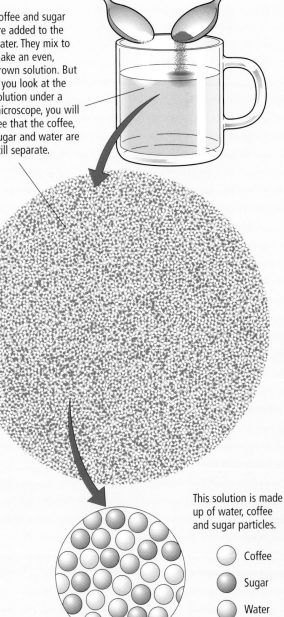

Coffee and sugar are added to the water. They mix to make an even, brown solution. But if you look at the solution under a microscope, you will see that the coffee, sugar and water are still separate.

This solution is made up of water, coffee and sugar particles.

○ Coffee
● Sugar
○ Water

▲▶ **Dissolve** – When you put a spoonful of instant coffee in a cup of clear, hot water, the coffee granules seem to disappear, and the water turns brown (above).

The brown colour is a clue to what has happened. Large granules of coffee have been pulled apart into tiny pieces and then scattered evenly within the water. This is also what happens when you add sugar.

Sugar and coffee are still in the water; the brown colour comes from the coffee granules. If you tasted the water, you would be able to taste both coffee and sugar. The coffee, the sugar and the water are still separate from one another; they only seem to have become part of the water (right). The coffee and the sugar are said to be dissolved in the water.

When a substance seems to disappear into a liquid, we say it has dissolved. The mixture it forms with the liquid is called a solution. The substance has become mixed in with the liquid.

Drinking water

Water that is safe to drink. Very strict regulations are in place in many countries to make sure that drinking water is of the highest quality and does not contain poisonous substances, pieces of soil, or **disease**-carrying organisms.

Drinking water has to be both clarified (made to look clean) and purified (disinfected) by the time it reaches taps. This is a complicated and expensive process. (*See also:* **Aquifer**; **Aqueduct**; **Clean water**; **Reservoir**; **Water supply**.)

Drought

An unusually long period without significant **rainfall**.

Some parts of the world, particularly between latitudes 10° and 35°, have a more variable rainfall pattern than others, and so they can be said to be more drought-prone. These places include the Sahel region of Africa just south of the Sahara Desert, southern Africa, northeast Brazil, Australia, southern California, the southwestern United States and India. Some places have seasons when rain never falls. They are called dry seasons, but they are not droughts. In these areas droughts occur in the rainy season when the rains do not fall as normal.

E

El Niño

A change in the tropical currents of the Pacific Ocean that prevents **ocean** water rising from the sea bed and providing the nourishment that **ocean life** needs (*see:* **Ocean currents**). This happens about once every five years, devastating ocean life and causing extensive climatic change.

▲ **Drinking water** – A sequence of settling and cleaning ponds and filter beds has to be used to make water fit to drink.

Erosion

The breakdown and removal of rock or soil – from a river bed, bank, or a sea **cliff** – by **water**.

Erosion may happen almost instantly, as in the case of a river scraping rock from its banks and carrying it away or a wave crashing against a cliff. It may also be a very slow process, such as when water causes rock to crack or break up (a process called weathering). In this case the disintegration of the rock is not followed immediately by movement. The broken material may simply form soil, and only many decades or centuries later is the soil carried away, perhaps by a river during a **flood**.

Direct river erosion of the river bed and banks is related to the energy of the water. Rivers reach their greatest energy during a flood, when there is a large amount of water moving at a high speed. At this time erosion can be severe and can lead to problems for people living close to a river.

There are many ways of trying to prevent erosion. One common way is to reinforce the outside banks of **meanders** with concrete. (*See also:* **Drainage**.)

Estuary

A drowned **river** valley in a coastal lowland area.

Drowning occurs either because the land is sinking or from a worldwide rise in sea level, such as after the last **Ice Age**. An estuary is a region of slack **water** where **fresh water** and **sea water** meet. It is very rich in wildlife. (*See also:* **Water life**.)

Evaporation

The change of **water** from liquid to **vapour** at temperatures below boiling.

Evaporation occurs because the energy in warm air or sunlight can provide enough heat for water molecules to break free of the liquid that binds them together. As each molecule breaks free, it becomes part of the water vapour in the air. In this way liquid is changed into gas. This is the process behind the drying of a puddle or of clothes on a line.

Evaporation depends on the air being able to take up water

F

Fall line

A region where **rivers** have **waterfalls** or **rapids** down their valleys.

Many cities on the East Coast of America are built on a fall line because that was as far inland as boats could navigate. Thus the location of many cities was determined by the waterfalls and rapids on the rivers.

▼ **Fall line** – A fall line separates the coastal plain of eastern America from the hills of the Appalachians. These are the Potomac Falls near Washington, DC.

▶ **Finger lake** – These are long finger lakes in the mountains of New Zealand.

Fan

(*See:* **Alluvial fan**.)

Finger lake, ribbon lake

A long **lake** that fills the bottom of a mountain valley. Some also have **dams** of moraine (rock and ice) at their ends (*see:* **Glacier**).

Fjord

A deep, narrow, **flooded river** mouth that was formed at the end of the last **Ice Age**.

Fjords (pronounced fee-ords) have such steep sides that rivers entering them often create spectacular **waterfalls**. Fjords are also extremely deep. In some parts of the world a fjord is called a sound.

Flash flood

A **flood** that occurs suddenly and without warning. Flash floods are common after torrential mountain thunderstorms. They affect mountain and desert valleys where soils are thin and cannot soak up the **rain**. As a result, the rain quickly flows into rivers.

molecules. That will only happen slowly in still air because the air in contact with the water will soon become full, or saturated, with water vapour. However, if there is a breeze, then new dry air will continually flow over the water surface and take up each new water molecule as it breaks free. (*See also:* **Transpire** and **Water cycle**.)

▶ **Evaporation** – When water evaporates, the molecules of the water acquire enough energy (from heating in a pan, warmth from the air, or sunlight) to break free of the water surface and float into the air as water vapour.

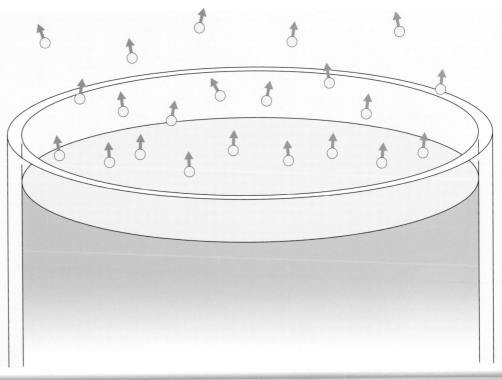

▶ **Flood** – A flooded airfield.

▼ **Flood** – A flood spills out to cover the flood plain. Many normal human activities are disrupted by this, especially communications.

Flood

When **water** flows across normally dry land. Both **rivers** and seas can cause flooding.

On either side of a **river channel** there is land which has been flattened by the river during previous floods. This is called a **flood plain**. Anything built on the flood plain – no matter how far it might be from the river – will be flooded from time to time.

Floods are not just water. All flood waters carry huge amounts of **sediment** with them. (*See also:* **Bore**; **Alluvium; Flash flood; Water cycle**.)

(*For flood prevention see:* **Barrage**; **Dam; Dike; Groyne; Levee; Reservoir**.)

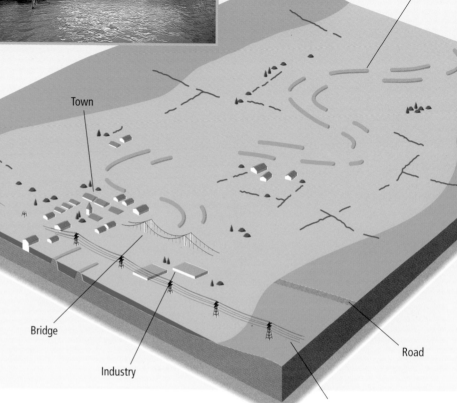

Levee

Town

Bridge

Industry

Road

Power cables

Flood plain

The flat land on either side of a **river** that is made of **alluvium** deposited by the river in times of **flood**.

Because flood plains are formed by the action of rivers and floods, they are liable to regular flooding. (*See also:* **Levee** and **Oxbow, oxbow lake**.)

▼ **Flood plain** – A flood plain is the flat land on either side of a river.

Flood plain

Levees

Ford

A part of a **river** where it is shallow enough to cross without a boat or a bridge.

Fords are often found in straight stretches of rivers away from bends. These are the places where the river is widest and the bed is an even depth. At bends the deepest water is found on the outside of the bend. (*See also:* **Braided river**.)

Fork

One of the **head waters** of a **river** system close to a **watershed** that is regarded as being the starting point of a river system. An alternative term is **branch**.

▲ **Ford** – This ancient ford allows travellers to cross the river. It is still used by local people when the river level is low.

Freezing point of water

0°C. The freezing point varies with the substances **dissolved** in the water. **Sea water**, for example, freezes at about –2°C, and very salty water may only freeze below –5 to –10°C. The freezing point of water is the same as the melting point of **ice**.

Fresh water

Water that contains less than 1g of **dissolved** salts per litre. Ninety-eight per cent of fresh liquid water is trapped in rocks as **ground water**. Only 2% is held in **rivers** and **lakes**. Nevertheless, river waters are being replenished faster than ground waters, so rivers represent a better sustainable **water supply** than ground water.

G

Geyser

A pulsating source of hot **water** that jets upwards from the ground to make a spectacular boiling fountain.

Geysers are produced when cold water seeps down into hot rocks and blocks already hot water from flowing to the surface.

When cold water flows down the same pipe that heated water is trying to use to reach the surface, the cold water acts like a lid, trapping the hot water, so that it becomes hotter and hotter. Eventually, the pressure of the

superheated water pushes the cold water out of the pipe, shooting it upwards as a fountain. Once the pressure has been released, the geyser stops and the cycle begins again.

Glacier

A river of **ice**. A valley glacier is a glacier that flows entirely within a valley. If a glacier comes out of the mountains and spreads out onto a plain, it becomes part of an ice sheet. (*See also:* **Crevasse**; **Ice crystals**; **Lake**.)

▲ **Glacier** – This is the snout, or end, of a glacier. The streaks on the glaciers are broken rock that has fallen onto the surface of the ice and is being carried with it. It is called a moraine.

Ground water

The **water** held within water-bearing rocks, or **aquifers**, in the ground.

Water may flow naturally to the surface and come out as a **spring** or bubble upwards as a flowing pool, or it may be taken out of the rocks by using a **well** or a bore hole. Limestone, chalk and sandstone are the main rocks that

▶ **Geyser** – Old Faithful geyser, Yellowstone National Park. It erupts a fountain of water about once every 50 minutes, hence its name.

▶ **Groyne** – The Rhine in Germany. The groynes are the low banks that stick out into the water on the far shore.

are **permeable** enough for ground water to flow through them readily. Water that is trapped in aquifers is called **artesian water**. It is a particularly important source of water in dry areas, but is exploited in all parts of the world. (*See also:* **Water cycle**.)

Groyne

A barrier placed in the bank of a **river** to prevent bank **erosion** and to keep **water** in the centre of the river when water levels are low. Groynes are also used on beaches that are liable to erosion. The groynes are built out from the shore, trapping **sand** that would otherwise be washed from the beach. Groynes are especially common close to towns where a beach is of major tourist importance.

H

Hardness

A measure of the amount of mineral matter, and in particular calcium bicarbonate, that is **dissolved** in **water**. Water is said to be hard if it is difficult to make soap lather. Water is said to be soft if soap lathers easily. The more bicarbonate dissolved in the water, the harder it is.

Because minerals are less soluble in hot water than in cold water,

▶ **Hardness** – In hard water areas, heating elements in hot water tanks quickly develop thick lime scale.

heating water causes some of the minerals to settle out. This produces the scaling seen on kettles and on the inside of hot-water pipes.

Hard water is produced when rain water percolates through limestone or chalk rocks. While it is percolating, the water dissolves some of the limestone (calcium carbonate), turning it into soluble calcium bicarbonate.

Water hardness can be beneficial to health, reducing the amount of heart disease.

People who want to reduce the hardness of water can use chemical filters. They work by causing a chemical reaction between the filtering chemical (often calcium hydroxide, slaked lime or sodium carbonate, soda ash) and the hard water.

Another method of removing hardness is to use a column of resin. This process (called ion exchange) uses sodium chloride (common salt).

Head

The height of the **water**, for example, in a tank or **reservoir** above the tap or drain where the water flows out. The higher the head of water, the greater the pressure on the water as it flows out of the tap, and the faster it flows.

Head water

One of the small streams that is at the start, or head, of a **river** system. Head water streams may be known as a **branch** or a **fork**.

Heat capacity

The ability of a substance to absorb or give out heat without changing temperature. It is measured as the ratio of heat absorbed by a material to its temperature change.

The heat capacity in calories per gram is called specific heat. The calorie is based on the specific heat of **water**, defined as the heat required to raise the temperature of one gram of water by one degree Celsius.

Water has the highest heat capacity of all common materials. The heat capacity of water is, for example, five times that of **sand**. This is an extremely important property. It explains why the **oceans** heat up slowly each summer and cool down slowly each winter.

The ability of water to absorb heat in all of its forms is important in the atmosphere. Water **vapour** in the air soaks up heat radiated from the ground and releases this heat slowly into the air. This slows the loss of heat into space. In this way the temperature of the atmosphere is kept 15°C higher than it would be if there was no water vapour present.

The high heat capacity of water also explains why the dry soil close to a pond heats up more quickly than the surface water of the pond and why people use water to store heat in

environmentally friendly central heating systems. Anywhere where heat needs to be stored, water is usually chosen.

Salty water has a slightly lower heat capacity than **fresh water** because the salt itself has a low heat capacity. (*See also:* **Water cycle**.)

Hot springs

Sources of warm **water** that flow naturally from the ground.

The warming effect is usually produced by the water flowing near areas of hot volcanic rock. Some hot springs have been harnessed for geothermal power (the production of electric power by using the steam from hot springs to turn the shaft of a generator).

(*See also:* **Sea water**.)

Humidity

The amount of water **vapour** in the air. The more water vapour, the higher the humidity. It is most usually expressed as relative humidity – the amount of **water** in the air compared to the maximum amount it could hold at that temperature. Air that has all of the water vapour it can absorb is said to be saturated and has a relative humidity of 100%. Air in a centrally heated home may only have a relative humidity of 20 to 30%.

▼ Hydroelectric power – Hydroelectric power is suited to naturally fast flowing rivers on steep slopes. A dam is built to create a pond. The outlet of the dam runs past the turbines. In this picture surplus water is being released from the top of the dam. It gives an idea of the immense power in falling water.

Hydroelectric power

Electricity produced by forcing **water** to turn turbine blades that are connected to a shaft that turns an electric generator.

Hydroelectricity is a clean form of power because it generates no waste gases and uses natural supplies of water. The only effect it has on the landscape is that water has to be stored behind **dams** so there can be a reliable supply of electricity (*see:* **Reservoir**).

Hydroelectric turbines are placed at the foot of a dam, not high up in it. This allows water to drop from a maximum height and therefore build up the greatest speed (*see:* **Head**).

It is also possible to generate hydroelectric power from **rivers** that flow slowly, as is done on rivers where there are **barrages**. However, to compensate for the lack of speed, large volumes of water have to flow past the turbine blades, so this system is only suited to large rivers. (*See also:* **Water power**.)

Hydrological cycle

A scientific term for the **water cycle**.

▶ **Ice** – Ice is one state of water. Ice will change state to liquid water as it melts. It will also change directly to water vapour, a process called sublimation.

I

Ice

The solid form of **water**. It can be produced by the **freezing** of liquid water or directly from **vapour** (a process called **sublimation**). Frozen water vapour is called frost when it is on the ground and **ice crystals** or snowflakes when formed in a cloud.

All ice crystals are single crystals, often with branching patterns. A single snowflake is a single ice crystal. Most 'snowflakes' are, in fact, groups, or aggregates, of snowflakes. When a body of liquid water such as a **river**, **lake**, or sea turns to ice, the surface freezes first. Even **raindrop** surfaces can freeze, in which case the frozen drops form hail. Partly melted ice crystals are called sleet. (*See also:* **Precipitation**.)

The largest amounts of solid ice are found in the world's ice sheets, most notably in Antarctica, Greenland and the Arctic Sea.

Ice conducts electricity much more easily than most solids. Only metals conduct electricity better.

The ice that grows from liquid water is a crystalline material that is made of interlocking crystals. Because the crystals do not have well-defined faces, as they do in snowflakes, this form of ice appears to be a transparent, featureless solid rather than having the shiny surface of a crystal. Scientists call it an amorphous solid. The same property is true of other transparent materials such as glass.

Ice will only melt when sufficient heat has been added. The heat needed for melting is called the latent heat of fusion. The temperature of the ice does not rise while heat is being absorbed in the melting process.

The amount of heat needed to melt a gram of ice is 337 joules (0.337 kilojoules) or 80 calories. This is a much higher amount of heat than is needed to melt most other solids. The fact that ice soaks up a lot of heat before it melts explains why ice packs are good for keeping things cool and why icebergs take such a long time to melt when they float into warm **oceans**.

Ice is only nine-tenths as dense as water because of the way ice forms into a network of crystals as it freezes. The expansion during ice formation has important results in many places. It explains why exposed water pipes burst on a cold winter night, why bottles of water crack when put in a freezer, and why blocks of rock are loosened from **cliffs** during the winter.

The melting temperature of ice decreases as more pressure is applied. This has important effects. It is well known that it is easy to skid on frozen roads. This is because ice has low friction, or stickiness. When ice is under pressure, for example, from the weight of a car tyre or the blade of an ice-skater, it melts and turns to water. The water then acts as a lubricant, causing the skidding. **Glaciers** move over their rocky beds for the same reason. (*See also:* **Crevasse**.)

Ice Age

A period when the world's climate cools and **glaciers** surge down from mountains to form **ice** sheets. At present, glaciers and ice sheets have shrunk back, but it is likely they will eventually grow again. (*See also:* **Fjord**; **Lake**; **Waterfall**.)

◀▲ **Ice crystals** – Ice crystals are typically six-sided or have six points.

Ice crystals

Water molecules are made of hydrogen and oxygen atoms. The molecule is arranged with one hydrogen atom at one end, the oxygen and the other hydrogen atom at the other end. The molecule is shaped just like a dumb-bell. The hydrogen end has a positive charge, while the hydrogen–oxygen end has a negative charge. Because of this, water molecules attract one another end-to-end. The attraction is called hydrogen bonding.

The shape of an ice crystal is due to these end-to-end links. The links make six-sided (hexagonal) rings of water molecules, and that is why ice crystals have six points.

▶ **Ice crystals** – This is a snowball made from compacted ice crystals.

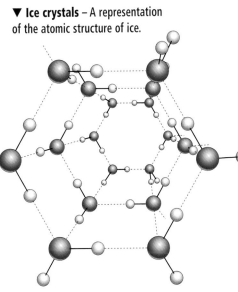

▼ **Ice crystals** – A representation of the atomic structure of ice.

The arrangement of water molecules in **ice** does not allow any space for any materials that were **dissolved** in the liquid water. As a result, these dissolved materials are ejected as ice forms, and even **sea water** (which contains much salt) produces pure ice. Indeed, the **freezing** of water can be used to make **drinking water** from sea water (a form of **desalinisation**).

Ice is a brittle solid. If it is struck with a hammer, it shatters. However, if pressure is applied for a long time, the ice will begin to change shape, and in the case of **glacier** ice it will flow like syrup.

Given enough time, each of the hexagonal layers of molecules in an ice crystal can glide past one another. Furthermore, in places where the ice pressure is extreme, such as where the ice rests on the bed of a glacier, the ice will melt, providing water for lubrication.

The greater the pressure, the more the sheets of molecules glide, and the faster the ice flows. As a result, the ice near the bottom of a glacier flows faster than the surface ice. The surface ice, which is not under much pressure, cracks, resulting in the formation of **crevasses**.

Irrigation

The supply of **water** to farmland so that crops can grow in areas where natural **water supplies** are scarce or unreliable.

Water for irrigation comes either from **ground water** supplies or from **reservoirs** and **river** diversions. (*See also:* **Aqueduct**.)

In dry countries irrigation can use more water than all other demands (home, industry, power) put together.

L

Lake

A body of still **water** not directly connected to the open **ocean**. Some large lakes are called seas (for example, the Aral Sea).

Most lakes were formed at the end of an **Ice Age**, when hollows scoured by former **glaciers** and **ice** sheets filled with water.

You can find lakes all over the world, but especially in regions that have been recently affected by an Ice Age, for example, northern Europe and North America. These kinds of lakes may be in glaciated valleys (*see:* **Finger lake**), or they may be in more low-lying regions. The Great Lakes of North America (Huron, Michigan, Superior, Ontario, Erie) are the world's largest lakes formed by glaciation. Lakes are also found in places where the land has sunk due to the splitting of the Earth's crust (for example, Lake Malawi in East Africa). Small lakes are also found in ancient volcanic cones. They are called **crater lakes** (for example, Crater Lake, Oregon).

◀ **Irrigation** – This picture shows centre pivot irrigation, where water is pumped from underground up a well and then used to irrigate a circular field through a large, rotating beam sprayer.

▼ **Irrigation** – This is what spray irrigation looks like from the ground.

Most lakes contain **fresh water**, but some inland lakes are salty. Examples of salty lakes include the Great Salt Lake of Utah. Very salty lakes that dry up from time to time, called **playa lakes**, are found in places where the lakes have no outlet, and where the rivers that drain into them cross beds of salty rock.

Lake Superior covers 82,100 sq km and is the largest lake in the world in terms of area. Lake Baikal in Siberia has the largest volume of water, some 23,000 cu km. The land with the largest density of lakes may be Finland, which has tens of thousands of small lakes. The country with the largest number of lakes may be Canada because it is the largest country to be glaciated.

Lakes are not formed by rivers and they do not last long compared with the history of the Earth. Most have a life of just a few hundred or a few thousand years. After that they become filled in with the **sediment** brought to them by inflowing rivers.

The upper parts of lakes are good for fish and other **water life** because there is light, oxygen, heat and nourishment brought in by rivers. But deeper waters have little light and less nourishment or oxygen, so the number of species is often small.

Lakes are not good at cleaning themselves. If they become **polluted** by sewage or waste from factories, the life in them may be threatened. Lake Erie, for example, is officially designated as a dead lake due to pollution.

Lakes are very important sources of water for cities, factories and **irrigation**. Where there are insufficient natural lakes, people often create them by building **dams**. An artificial lake is called a **reservoir**.

Lakes are also often used for transportation, connecting cities that lie on opposite sides of the lake.

▲ **Lake** – This image from space shows Lake Titicaca, Bolivia and Peru, the largest lake in South America.

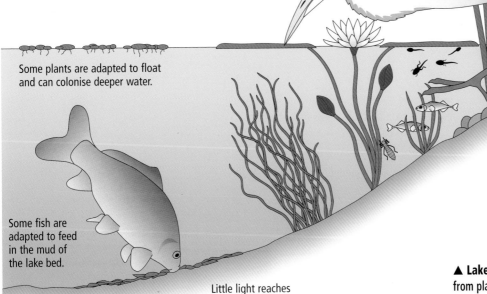

Some plants are adapted to float and can colonise deeper water.

Some fish are adapted to feed in the mud of the lake bed.

Little light reaches the lake floor.

On unexposed shores plants thrive in the sunlit shallows. It is these lake edges that have the highest density of animals and plants.

▲ **Lake** – Lakes support a wide range of life, from plants, fish and insects, to amphibians and to birds like herons.

Levee

A natural or artificial embankment or **dike** that runs along both sides and parallel to a **river channel**. The levee traps the **river** into a narrow channel at all times except during the highest **floods**.

Natural levees are built up during floods as rivers flow out from their channels. **Water**, including much suspended **silt** and **sand**, flows from the fast-moving channel to the relatively slow-moving areas of the **flood plain**. As a result, the silt and sand are quickly dropped and build up into long ridges. (*See also:* **Groyne**.)

Lock

A gated device for allowing boats to navigate around weirs, **barrages** and other obstacles along a **river**.

Melting point of ice

(*See:* **Freezing point of water**.)

Moisture

The amount of **water** held in the air as invisible water **vapour**. In this state water is a gas.

The amount of moisture in the air varies with the temperature of the air. Hot air can hold more moisture than cool air.

For example, when air flows towards a mountain, it rises up the mountain side and cools. Because the cooler air holds less moisture, it starts to release surplus moisture as droplets or **ice crystals**, and this produces a cloud. When the droplets group together, they become **rain** or snow.

O

Oasis

A reliable natural **spring** in a desert.

Oases are fed by springs flowing from rocks. The source of the spring may be hundreds of kilometres away from the spring in a place where **water** is more plentiful, such as a mountain range.

Many oases are very small, but some can be hundreds of square kilometres in area.

M

Meander

A part of a **river** with regular bends.

A meander continually changes shape as the fast-flowing current of **water** swirls around the outside of the bend, eroding the outside bank. At the same time, slack water on the inside of the bend lets **silt** drop out. Because **erosion** occurs on one side of a meander bend and silt falls on the other, the channel stays the same width even though the bend keeps moving across a **flood plain**. (*See also:* **Cliff, river cliff**.)

The pattern, shape and size of meanders vary with the steepness of the river course and the amount of water flowing.

Meanders can develop very pronounced loops called **oxbows**.

Meanders increase the length of a river and make river transportation less efficient. Many meanders have been cut through to create shortcuts on the world's largest navigable rivers, most notably on the Mississippi River below Greenville, Mississippi. (*Compare with:* **Braided river**.)

Scouring of the outside of a bend produces a steep slope called a river cliff.

▲ **Meander** – A section of river showing how water flows around the outside of each bend, scouring on the inside and transferring material to the inside.

Corkscrew flow of water carries the scoured material to the slack waters of the inside of the bend, where they settle to the bottom.

▶ **Meander** – Meanders are the natural winding of a river over a flood plain. The river cliffs are on the outside of each bend. Notice how the insides of the bends have plants growing on them. That is where the sand and mud have recently been laid down. (Inset) The location of the main current at each bend.

Ocean

A large body of salt **water** that is not enclosed by land. Parts of oceans that are partly cut off from the open ocean by fingers of land or islands are called seas.

Ocean water contains about 35g of **dissolved** salts per litre (*see:* **Sea water**). This is too high an amount for people to drink or for most plants to use.

The oceans occupy 71% of the surface of the Earth. They have a total volume of 1,370 million cu km. The average depth of the world's oceans is 3,800m. Only about 1% of the ocean floor lies below 6,000m, and it is confined to narrow arc-shaped trenches that lie mainly on the edges of the Pacific Ocean. They are places where the ocean floor is sinking below the surrounding continent as part of the process called plate tectonics.

Elsewhere the sea floor begins with a gentle slope. This flat shallow area is called the continental shelf and is up to 150m deep. Beyond the continental shelf is a steeper slope, called the continental slope, that leads down to the true ocean floor, called the abyssal plain. In the centre of some oceans are long, mainly submerged, mountain chains. The largest of them is the Mid-Atlantic Ridge, the longest mountain range in the world. It is made entirely of volcanoes, very few of which rise to the surface of the sea. Those that do rise to the surface form volcanic islands.

The ocean ridges play an important role in shaping the pattern of **ocean currents**.

The **sediments** carried by rivers on land drift out to sea and settle on the ocean floor, where they build up to form layers of sediment that will eventually compress into new rock.

The continual movement of the world's land surface causes oceans to form and close. It is likely that no current ocean is older than 100 million or so years. (*See also:* **Ocean life**; **Tide**; **Water cycle**.)

Ocean currents

The **waters** of the **oceans** are not still, but are continually moving. The patterns of this movement are the ocean currents.

Water moves in the oceans because it is driven by the winds. Water also moves because some regions are more dense (saltier) than others.

The warmest parts of the oceans are in the tropics, and the coldest are near the poles.

The saltiest parts of the oceans are at the same latitudes as the world's great deserts. Between about 15° and 20° of latitude there is almost no **rain**, but the sea is continually losing water by **evaporation**.

In contrast, near the equator, where rain falls every day, and in high latitudes where there are storms, **fresh water** is continually added to the sea and the water is less salty.

As water moves to balance out differences in the heat and saltiness, it is affected by the spinning of the Earth. The spinning of the Earth causes the ocean currents to turn clockwise in the Northern Hemisphere and counter-clockwise in the Southern Hemisphere. As a result, ocean currents tend to move in circles around the edges of the oceans.

The movements of the currents become concentrated in some parts of the oceans. One of the most noticeable currents is called the North Atlantic Drift, or the Gulf Stream. It begins in the Gulf of Mexico, flows up the East Coast of the United States, and then heads off across the North Atlantic Ocean to reach the western shores of Europe. The heat that this current carries is enormous and accounts for the fact that the winter climate in western Europe is much milder than on the eastern seaboard of North America.

In other places cold currents rise to the surface and cool the air. This is very noticeable in places such as the coast of California. (*See also:* **El Niño**.)

▼ **Ocean currents** – Ocean currents change position during the year, but much more slowly than changes in the atmosphere. You can see the changes in the pattern off the coast of North America between February (top) and August (bottom).

Cold ocean current

Warm ocean current

Ocean life

The **oceans** contain more life than anywhere else on Earth. Indeed, it is believed that life began in the world's oceans.

The oceans are full of plant life. However, unlike on land where the plant life is easy to see and makes up a striking part of the landscape, the plant life in the oceans may go unnoticed. That is because it is mainly composed of microscopic living organisms called plankton that drift near the surface of the ocean waters. They absorb sunlight just like land plants and use it, along with the carbon dioxide

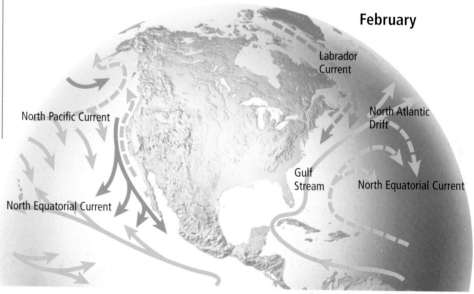

February

Labrador Current

North Pacific Current

North Atlantic Drift

Gulf Stream

North Equatorial Current

North Equatorial Current

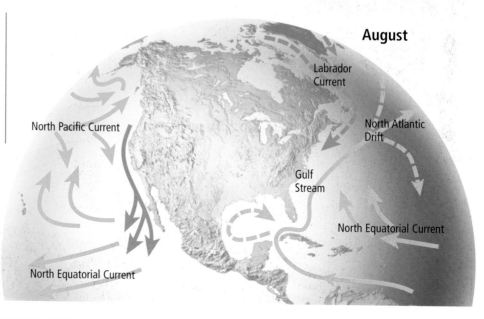

August

Labrador Current

North Pacific Current

North Atlantic Drift

Gulf Stream

North Equatorial Current

North Equatorial Current

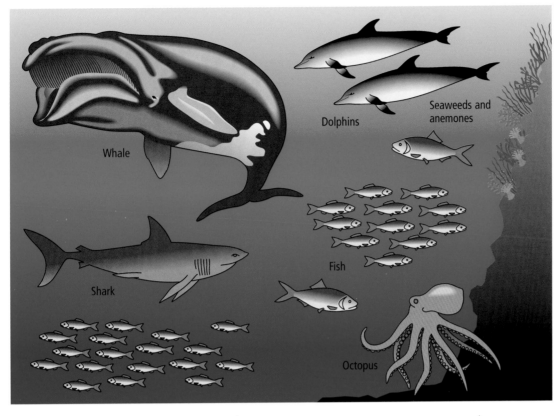

Dolphins

Seaweeds and anemones

Whale

Shark

Fish

Octopus

◄ **Ocean life** – Oceans have a greater amount of life than the land. The bottom of the food chain is mainly microscopic plankton. This provides the food for invertebrates such as molluscs, fish and for mammals such as whales.

dissolved in the water, to make their tissues. At the same time, they give out oxygen, which aerates the water and makes it possible for other life to survive.

The ocean waters also contain all of the nourishment that plants need to develop their tissues, although it may be concentrated in some places more than others. One place where nourishment is plentiful is where **ocean currents** rise from

the sea bed to the surface. Such places contain more life than anywhere else in the world. A good example is the Peru Current off western South America, where the prevailing winds bring deep water towards the surface. When this up-welling occurs, plankton thrive and the fish and other animals that depend on them for food also grow in enormous numbers. (*See also:* **El Niño**; **Sea water**; **Water life**.)

Oxbow, oxbow lake

A bend in a meandering **river** that almost doubles back on itself and leaves only a narrow neck of land between parts of the channel (*see:* **Meander**).

An oxbow lake is a small arc-shaped depression, often containing a crescent-shaped **lake**. It represents an abandoned oxbow, part of the former course of a river where the narrow neck has been cut right through.

Oxbows are only found on river **flood plains**. For photographs of oxbows see page 30. (*See also:* **Billabong**.)

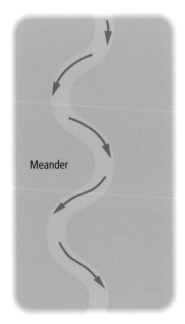

Meander

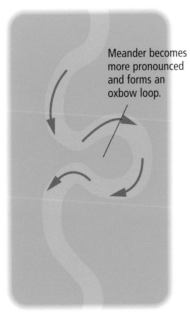

Meander becomes more pronounced and forms an oxbow loop.

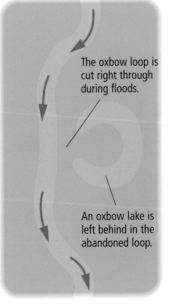

The oxbow loop is cut right through during floods.

An oxbow lake is left behind in the abandoned loop.

◄ **Oxbow, oxbow lake** – Oxbows develop as meanders double back on themselves. The diagram sequence at left shows how a meander can then be cut off to create an oxbow lake.

Permeable rock

▼ **Oxbow** – An oxbow at Stirling, Scotland.

▼ **Oxbow** – An oxbow cut off on the Green River, Utah.

P

Permeable rock

A rock that **water** can flow through easily.

There are many types of rock that water can flow through. Some, like sandstone and chalk, have small connecting spaces called pores that water can flow through. Others, like limestone, have no spaces for water inside the rock, but they are broken into large blocks, and the water flows between the blocks. (*See also:* **Aquifer** and **Porous**).

Playa, playa lake

A desert **lake**, often dry and marked by white salt crusts. Playas are formed in the centre of inland **drainage basins**. The minerals **dissolved** in the rock of the surrounding land are washed into the lake by **rain**. When the rain water evaporates, the minerals are left behind as sparkling white sheets (*see:* **Evaporation**).

Polluted water

All **water** contains some **dissolved** chemicals. Therefore, no naturally occurring water is absolutely pure. Polluted water is defined as water that contains sufficient impurities to make it unfit for its intended use.

There are many causes of water pollution, but it is usually defined as a high level of impurities as a result of human action.

Most water pollution is caused when contaminated water seeps from a concentrated source into **rivers**, **lakes**, or **ground water** reserves.

The three main sources of pollution are sewage, fertilisers and industrial wastes (usually metal compounds).

Poor people living close to a river often deposit all of their wastes in the river because they have no alternative. These human wastes are very rich in nitrogen and phosphorus. In the countryside farmers use high quantities of nitrogen and phosphorus fertilisers. Both nitrogen and phosphorus are soluble and are carried by water through the soils and into rivers. This provides an excess of the nourishment that microscopic water plants (algae) need and so they grow rapidly. As they grow, they remove oxygen from the water, making it impossible for other forms of life to exist.

In industrialised countries rivers often become polluted by industrial wastes. These wastes often contain metals that are poisonous both to river life and to people. (*Compare with:* **Clean water**.)

Porous rock

A rock containing many small spaces, or pores.

The main porous rocks that conduct **water** and are also **permeable** are chalk and sandstone. Water seeps into, and flows through, them easily.

A porous rock may hold water but not allow water to flow through it. **Clay** is an example of this type of rock. Although clay has pores, it is not permeable.

► **Polluted water** – A river polluted with industrial waste, including heavy metals and detergents.

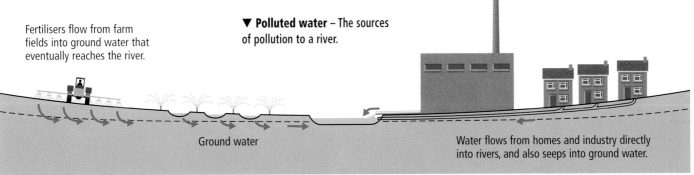

Fertilisers flow from farm fields into ground water that eventually reaches the river.

▼ **Polluted water** – The sources of pollution to a river.

Ground water

Water flows from homes and industry directly into rivers, and also seeps into ground water.

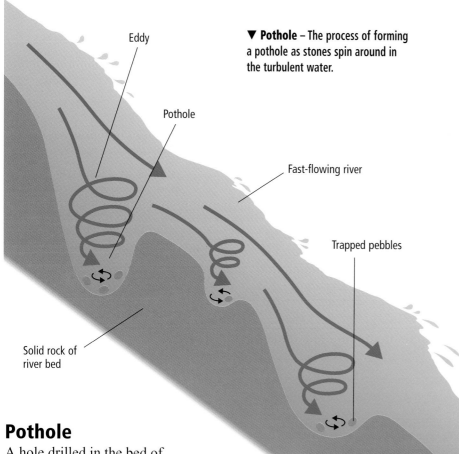

Eddy

Pothole

▼ **Pothole** – The process of forming a pothole as stones spin around in the turbulent water.

Fast-flowing river

Trapped pebbles

Solid rock of river bed

▲ **Pothole** – River bed pothole with some of the pebbles that scoured it.

Pothole

A hole drilled in the bed of a fast-flowing **river**. This can only happen in a river that has a rocky bed and is carrying pebbles or larger materials. As the **water** swirls around, it forms natural whirlpools or eddies in which pebbles become trapped. As they bump against the rocky bed, they rub it away, forming a depression that tends to make the whirlpool more permanent. Eventually, deep potholes can be drilled this way.

Pothole is also used as a term for a hollow where a stream disappears into a **permeable rock**, such as limestone, although it should correctly be called a 'swallow hole'.

Precipitation

Any liquid or solid **water** that comes from the air and wets the ground. The forms of precipitation include dew, drizzle, hail, **ice**, **rain**, sleet and snow.

Precipitation begins when air cools to a point at which it can no longer hold water as **vapour**. At this point **condensation** occurs and liquid water droplets form. If the air is very cold, **ice crystals** form instead of water droplets. The droplets or ice crystals that form in the air are minute and mainly grow around small particles of dust. When large numbers of these droplets form, they partly obscure the sky and are seen as cloud.

The formation of droplets or ice crystals in the air does not usually lead to precipitation. For that to happen, the droplets or ice crystals have to come together and form large masses that can fall out against the natural up-draught of air in a cloud.

The stronger the up-draught, the bigger the water droplet or snowflake has to be before it falls.

The biggest droplets (and partly frozen droplets called hailstones) come from giant thunderstorms, since they have the strongest up-draughts.

Some forms of precipitation do not come from water or snow falling from clouds. Dew forms directly on a cold surface when air near the ground cools. If the air is very cold, a thin sheet of ice (called black ice) or a layer of ice crystals (called frost) can form.

R

Rain, raindrop, rainfall

Droplets of **moisture** that have become big enough to fall out of clouds. It is one form of **precipitation**. (*See also:* **Water cycle**.)

▶ **Rain** – Torrential rainfall during an Indian monsoon.

Rainshadow

The way that a mountain range blocks the path of air and forces it to rise and release its **moisture** on the windy side, leaving very little moisture on the side sheltered from the wind. That side is the rainshadow side of the mountain.

Rapids

Fast-flowing stretches of **water** formed where the **river** surface breaks up into waves because rocks are near the surface. For this to happen, the river must flow over beds of rocks that are jutting upwards.

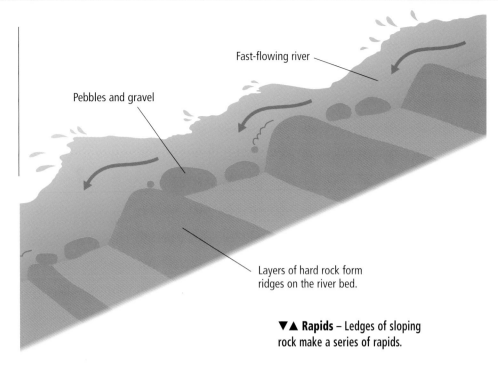

Fast-flowing river

Pebbles and gravel

Layers of hard rock form ridges on the river bed.

▼▲ **Rapids** – Ledges of sloping rock make a series of rapids.

Many rapids are used as recreational areas for white-water rafting. (*See also:* **Cataract** and **Fall line**.)

Reservoir

An artificial **lake** created by building a **dam** across a **river**. Some reservoirs are called lakes because of their size.

River flows naturally vary through the year, so that there may be more **water** than can be used at one time of year and too little at another. During periods of heavy **rainfall** rivers may also swell, burst their banks and **flood**, leading to widespread destruction. Reservoirs are built to control the flow of water in a river to prevent flooding and to ensure a reliable flow of water through the year.

Reservoirs are used to provide **drinking water**, for **irrigation** water and to generate **hydroelectric power**.

Reservoir sites have to be chosen with care because they take up a large amount of land that cannot then be used for other purposes. Ideally, sites are chosen where a

dam can be built across a deep, narrow valley. This means that the cost of building the dam is kept as low as possible, while the steep, narrow valley will use up a minimum of land. A further advantage is that the surface area is small compared with the volume of water, so in hot weather the amount of water lost by **evaporation** is kept low.

Because reservoirs are regions of still water in the path of a river, when the river enters the reservoir, any **sediment** it is carrying will settle out. Over time, this will fill in the lake. It is, therefore, important to build reservoirs on rivers that do not have a high sediment load.

Most reservoirs have a useful lifespan of less than 150 years. After this they contain too much sediment to work properly. Those reservoirs located on rivers with a high **silt** load may only last for a few decades.

▶ **Reservoir** – Reservoirs can be enlargements of existing lakes, or they can be flooded river valleys. Reservoirs on flat land may need to be enclosed on all sides by a wall called a bund.

Ribbon lake
(*See:* **Finger lake**.)

River
A naturally winding channel that drains surplus **water** from a **drainage basin**. (Small rivers are called streams and brooks).

At any one moment the world's rivers carry only one-ten-thousandth of 1% of the water that exists in the **oceans** and in the atmosphere of the Earth. But this amount, some 40,000 cubic kilometres a year, is usually enough to provide the world's people with all the water they need.

A river is part of the **water cycle**. It carries the water that has fallen as **rain** or has melted from snow back to the oceans, where it **evaporates** to make rain once more. As this water flows back to the sea, it has the energy to pick up and carry loose material. This material is called **sediment**. (*See also:* **Abrasion**; **Alluvium**; **Attrition**.)

As a river flows, it shapes land by cutting down into its bed. If no other **erosion** happened, as is the case when a river flows through a desert, the river cuts a gorge. A river by itself cannot cut a valley; that is the result of a combination of river erosion and other processes such as landslides.

▲ **River** – A river is a place where water flows in a channel.

World's longest rivers

River	Drains into	Length (km)
Nile	Mediterranean Sea	6,650
Amazon	South Atlantic Ocean	6,400
Yangtze	East China Sea	6,300
Mississippi	Gulf of Mexico	5,971
Yenisey	Kara Sea	5,540
Huang Ho (Yellow)	Gulf of Chihli	5,464
Ob-Irtysh	Gulf of Ob	5,410
Paraña	South Atlantic Ocean	4,880
Congo	South Atlantic Ocean	4,700
Amur	Sea of Okhotsk	4,444

Rivers have been important throughout the history of exploration because they have provided one of the easiest means of moving through undeveloped country.

The amount of water in a river is a balance between what flows in and what flows out. The water flowing in comes mainly through the soil and the rock below the river bed. Very little of it falls directly onto the river as rain. In mountain areas some water may also come from melting snow and **ice**. During a heavy storm rain may fall faster than it can seep into the soil, and then it will flow over the surface and into rivers.

Rivers may lose water as they flow over **permeable rocks** and through evaporation. In developed areas large losses may also be due to the removal of water for human use.

Rivers flow in two patterns – a single winding channel, called a meandering channel (*see:* **Meander**) and a network of intertwined channels, called a **braided** channel.

(*For other natural river features see:* **Alluvial fan**; **Basin**; **Branch**; **Cataract**; **Cliff**; **Confluence**; **Delta**; **Drainage basin**; **Estuary**; **Ford**; **Fork**; **Head water**; **Oxbow, oxbow lake**; **Rapids**; **River channel**; **Tributary**; **Waterfall**.)

River channel

The trench in which a **river** flows for most of the year.

River channels change shape mainly during **floods**, when the channels are full of fast-flowing **water**, and the available energy is high. That happens on average about once every two or three years. For the rest of the time little change occurs. Two types of channel are the most common:

deep, winding or **meandering** channels that occur in places where the majority of the material carried is fine **sediment** such as **silt** and **clay**; and shallow, wide, **braided** channels that occur where the material is mainly **sand**, gravel, or cobbles.

Sand

A type of **sediment** carried by flowing **water**. It is between 0.06mm and 2mm across.

Runoff

Water that reaches a **river** as a result of **rainfall** or snow-melt in the river **basin**. It is part of the **water cycle**.

Runoff is mostly unseen, occurring as seepage through soil and rocks. Rain only flows directly to rivers after torrential rain or very long periods of rain. That is when **floods** occur.

Surface runoff is now much more common than it was in the past, mainly because people change the natural process that allows runoff to soak into the ground by

covering the ground with pavement and buildings. In such developed areas there is no chance for water to seep into the soil, and all of the rainfall becomes runoff. Moreover, the roofs and streets of cities are smooth and so do not hold back water.

To collect the water from roofs and streets, a complicated network of underground water-pipes is used. They are often called storm drains. Many such drains carry water directly to rivers and as a result rivers fill with water far more easily than in the past.

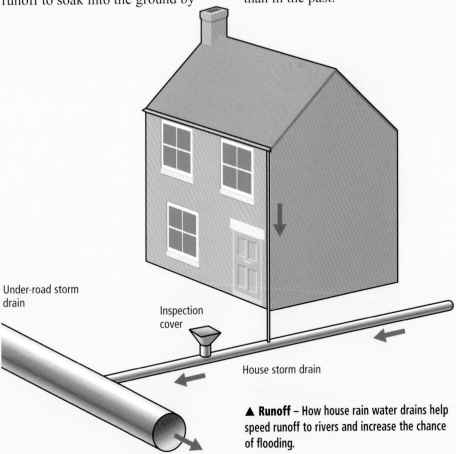

Under-road storm drain

Inspection cover

House storm drain

▲ **Runoff** – How house rain water drains help speed runoff to rivers and increase the chance of flooding.

Sea water

A solution of many different substances **dissolved** in **water**. The majority of the dissolved material is salt, but sea water contains many other substances that are vital for **ocean life**, including oxygen, nitrogen and carbon.

The sea contains an average of 35g of salt in each kilogramme of water. However, near river mouths, near the equator, and in high latitudes **rainfall** and **fresh water** dilute the sea slightly. In contrast, in the subtropics the sea is saltier than average due to the large amount of water that **evaporates** under the hot, sunny skies. (*See also:* **Desalinisation**.)

Most of the dissolved minerals in sea water are brought in by **rivers**. Rivers also carry large amounts of **sediment**. The sediment gradually

settles out of the sea water. More minerals are introduced into the sea through **hot springs** in the sea bed. These springs are known as hydrothermal vents.

Many of the minerals are used to make the skeletons of sea creatures. When these creatures die, their skeletons sink to the sea floor and consolidate as rock.

It is believed that the Earth's **oceans** began in the air. Very early in the history of the Earth, the planet condensed from the cold dust of space, then heated up and became molten, expelling gases that included water **vapour**.

It took hundreds of millions of years before the temperature of the air cooled below 100°C. But once this temperature had been reached, water condensed out of the air to form a very hot ocean. It was also

▲ Sea water – Salt is one of the valuable minerals that can be recovered from sea water by evaporation.

a very acid ocean and the acids in the water reacted with the rocks of the Earth's crust. It was during this time of chemical reactions that the chloride in hydrochloric acid formed a compound with the sodium in the crustal rocks to produce the salt (sodium chloride) that is now found in ocean water. So, even at this early stage the ocean became salty. Since this time some of the salt has been turned into rock salt, and so the modern ocean is only about half as salty as the early ocean.

The main chemical parts of sea water are chloride, sulphate, bicarbonate, bromide, fluoride, sodium, magnesium, calcium, potassium and strontium.

The pressure in the oceans rises one atmosphere for every 10m of depth.

The **freezing point** of sea water becomes lower as the salinity becomes higher. Sea water typically freezes at –2°C. The colder and saltier water is, the more dense it becomes and the more it tends to sink.

Sea water does not have a freezing pattern like fresh water. Fresh water is most dense at 4°C. When it freezes, it becomes less dense (the reason why **ice** floats on water). Sea water, on the other hand, continues to increase in density all the way down to its freezing point.

Sea water and the air above it are continually exchanging gases, including water vapour. However, the proportions of each gas in the air are different from those in the sea because some gases in the air are more soluble in water than others. Oxygen is very soluble in water and the percentage of oxygen in water is about one and a half times as great as the percentage of oxygen in the air.

The amounts of carbon dioxide and oxygen in sea water are also greatly affected by sea life because animals use oxygen and give out carbon dioxide, whereas plants use carbon dioxide and give out oxygen.

The sea appears blue. That is because light entering the water is scattered by the water so that more red light is absorbed than blue. If the sea appears green, that is due to a large number of microscopic plankton in the water, which are yellow. The combination of blue and yellow makes the green colour.

The occasional growth of vast numbers of plankton make the sea appear red. The Red Sea derives its name from this phenomenon, which is common there.

▲ **Sediment** – This picture shows a river carrying so much sediment in suspension that it has turned the water light grey. A tributary enters, carrying little sediment and is a clearer dark blue. The waters only mix much further downstream.

Sediment

Material that has been carried by **rivers** and then deposited. Sediment that has settled out on a river bed or **flood plain** may also be called **alluvium**.

Sediment can be large, in which case it is called **boulders**, cobbles and pebbles; it may be of medium size – gravel and **sand**; it may be fine – **silt**; or very fine – **clay** or mud.

The finest materials are carried in **suspension** and do not easily settle out on the bottom of the river. The medium-sized materials

only move during times when the river is full of water, and then they mostly hop along the river bed. The largest sediment moves only in times of **flood**, and then it rolls along the river bed. (*See also:* **Delta** and **Pothole**.)

▶ **Sediment** – This is suspended sediment. The silt has settled out, leaving the clay to colour the water.

Silt

Fine rock grains between 0.06mm and 0.0002mm across. Silt grains lie between **sand** and **clay** in size. Silt grains are easily carried by flowing **water**.

Silt is only common in **rivers** in some parts of the world. It is often found in rivers that flow over dry landscapes. Silt makes up nearly two-thirds of the **sediment** carried by the Mississippi River.

Silt is hard to tell from mud except by feel. Mud is sticky and clings together, but silt is slippery and feels like soap.

The word silt is also commonly used instead of **alluvium**. However, it is not an accurate use of the word.

Softness
(*See:* **Hardness**.)

Spring

A place where **water** naturally seeps or gushes from the ground.

Springs are fed by **ground water**. They occur in **aquifers**, often where a **river** cuts down to the **water table**. Other springs happen where a **permeable rock** is underlaid by an impermeable rock. This sometimes gives rise to 'weeping cliffs', as water seeps from the base of the permeable rock.

Bubbling or swiftly flowing springs are not especially common. Most rivers begin with muddy patches on a hillside rather than a bubbling spring. Bubbling springs are only possible where the rock below is highly permeable, such as chalk or limestone, or where it is

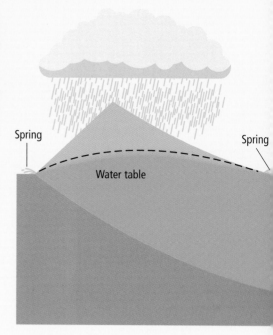

Spring

Spring

Water table

highly fractured, such as close to a volcano. (*See also:* **Hot spring** and **Oasis**.)

Solvent

A substance in which other materials **dissolve**. **Water** is the world's most common solvent. Even clear tap water, for example, contains a wide range of dissolved minerals, as a glance at the inside of a kettle will show. Some of the minerals are precipitated onto the surface of the kettle as the water is boiled.

▶ **Solvent** – Water is an excellent solvent. This can be seen by evaporating sea water and watching the salts come out of solution to make white rings on the surface of the container.

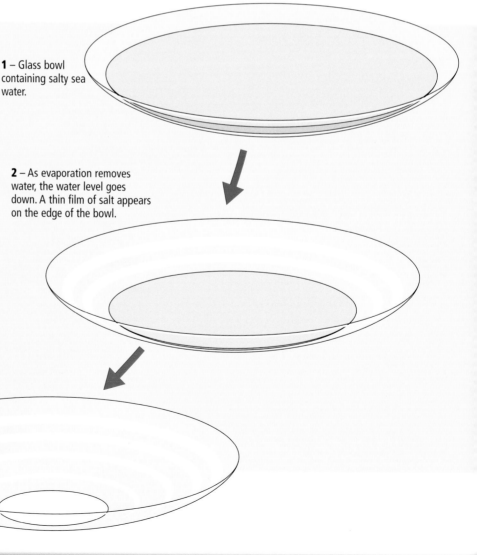

1 – Glass bowl containing salty sea water.

2 – As evaporation removes water, the water level goes down. A thin film of salt appears on the edge of the bowl.

3 – Evaporation is complete. Only the dissolved solids remain.

Sound
(*See:* **Fjord**.)

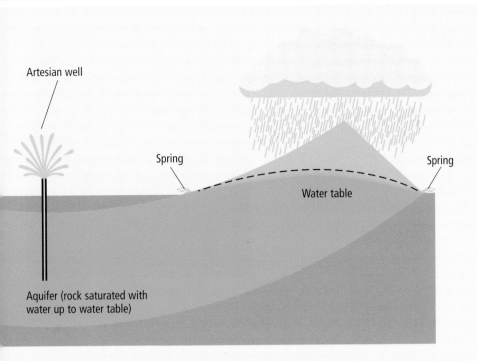

Artesian well

Spring

Spring

Water table

Aquifer (rock saturated with water up to water table)

▲ **Spring** – Springs occur where an aquifer reaches the surface. They often make lines called spring lines. In the past they provided clean water supplies and were favoured places for locating a village.

Steam

Water **vapour**. It is an odourless and colourless (and thus invisible) gas. Because steam occurs in air that is colder than the steam, some of the vapour immediately **condenses** and forms tiny **water** droplets. They are then visible and give steam a smoky appearance.

Steam occurs naturally when superheated water trapped in rocks deep underground finds a quick route to the surface. The water rushes to the surface, and because it is now under less pressure, it immediately begins to boil and turn to steam.

A **geyser** is a very good example of natural steam, but steam also occurs in places where there are **hot springs**, fumaroles and mud pools. Huge amounts of steam are also released during every volcanic eruption. The released water vapour cools in the air above the erupting volcano, turns into cloud and releases torrential **rain**.

Steam is used for many industrial purposes, but the most important use is to drive the turbines that are connected to electricity generators.

Steam for driving turbines is produced by heating water using coal, oil or natural gas, wood, refuse, solar power, or through nuclear reactions.

The steam is confined until it has built up considerable pressure, and then it is released into the turbine housing as a jet powerful enough to turn the turbine blades.

Steam is also used in many other industrial processes, for example, in refining petroleum and in making many metals.

In the home, steam is used for ironing, for removing wallpaper, and in the form of pressure for cooking food faster than at normal air pressure.

▲ **Steam** – When water boils, it forms a colourless vapour. What we usually call steam is, in fact, steam that has cooled and condensed back into tiny droplets. It is the droplets of water we see, not the steam. In this picture the true steam lies just beyond the kettle spout.

Sublimation

The change from water **vapour** to **ice** and vice versa. Normally, a substance changes from a solid, to a liquid, and then to a gas, but in certain circumstances it will change directly from a gas to a solid or from a solid to a gas. This happens, for example, in very cold clouds, where water vapour sublimes to make **ice crystals**.

Surface tension

The property of some liquids to cling together and make a film. It occurs when the molecules in the liquid are more strongly attracted to one another than to the air. In **water** the attraction is so strong that water film will crawl up the sides of a narrow tube.

Some water-borne animals, such as water boatmen, use the property of surface tension to walk on water.

Suspension

One of the several ways in which **water** can carry material (*see:* **Sediment**). **Silt** and **clay** are both carried in suspension in a fast-flowing **river**. They are responsible for the colour of the water.

Swamp

Places with waterlogged ground, mainly found in tropical and subtropical regions.

Because of the waterlogged conditions, the plants that grow in swamps have a particular range of adaptations, including the ability to absorb oxygen through their roots. All swamps have visible standing **water** and are dominated by trees. (Compare this with a marsh, which is dominated by grasses and a **bog**, which does not appear waterlogged until the soil is walked on.)

(*See also:* **Wetlands**.)

▲ **Swamp** – A cyprus swamp in Louisiana.

T

Tide

The rhythmic change in sea level that occurs due to the varying gravitational attraction of the Moon for the world's **ocean** waters. Tides, therefore, change with the relative positions of the Earth and the Moon.

Transpire

The process by which plants lose **water** to the air through the pores on the surfaces of their leaves.

Transpiration is an important process for plants. It helps keep leaves cool, and it removes water from the top of the plant so that more water-containing nutrients can be sucked up by the roots. Water is lost from the plant surface by **evaporation**. (*See also:* **Water cycle**.)

Tributary

A stream or **river** that feeds into a larger river. The small tributaries close to a **watershed** that eventually come together to form a major river are also often called **branch** or **fork**. The place where a tributary meets a main river is called the **confluence**.

Falling raindrop

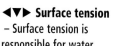

◄▼► **Surface tension** – Surface tension is responsible for water droplets and bubbles in soapy water.

V

Vapour, water vapour

Water when it is an invisible gas. The amount of water vapour that air can hold depends on the pressure and temperature of the air. In general, the cooler the air, the less water vapour it can hold. When the amount of water vapour in the air is as high as it can go, and the air can hold no more water vapour, we say the air is saturated. If saturated air cools, it will not be able to hold all of the water as vapour, and some will be condensed into liquid water droplets (*see:* **Condensation**). It will then be seen as cloud, fog, or dew. (*See also:* **Moisture** and **Steam**.)

Water vapour in the air

Water is moved from **oceans** to clouds as water vapour. The amount of water in the air is about one-thousandth of 1% of all the water in the oceans. The amount of vapour that air can hold depends on its temperature. Warm air can hold more vapour than cold air, so the amount of vapour in the air is much higher in the tropics than near the poles. The amount of water vapour in the air also changes between ground level and high altitudes. In fact, the air is so cold at 15km above the surface of the Earth that it holds almost no water vapour at all.

On average, water that has evaporated from the oceans will remain in the air as vapour for about 10 days before it forms into droplets or **ice crystals** and returns to the oceans of the land as **rain** or snow (*see:* **Evaporation** and **Sublimation**). Winds in the atmosphere can carry this vapour for thousands of kilometres during this time. (*See also:* **Water cycle**.)

W

Water

One of the world's most common substances, water can be found as solid **ice**, as liquid water and as water **vapour** (gas).

Water is a simple substance; each water molecule is made up of hydrogen and oxygen, hence its chemical formula, H_2O (two atoms of hydrogen, bonding with one atom of oxygen).

Water is a colourless, tasteless and odourless substance. It is found as both liquid and vapour (in the air) at room temperatures.

Water is a vital part of life. It is the major component in most cells of all living things, including animal blood and plant sap.

One of water's most useful features (and used by all living things) is its ability to **dissolve** substances and thereby carry them.

Nearly all the water in the world is a solution of water with other

substances dissolved in it. Pure water is extremely rare, but can be specially prepared, as distilled water.

Water is a dense substance. One old adage said, 'A pint of water weighs a pound and a quarter'. Nowadays we would say that 1 litre of water weighs a kilogramme. However it is measured, the weight (density) of water is often important. Water has a high density, which is why water soaked into clothes makes them heavy. The water accumulated behind a **dam** can be heavy enough to burst the dam unless it is very strong. The weight of water can be used instead of concrete in a garden roller. The work needed to carry a bucket full of water is considerable, which is why people in developing world countries, who have to carry their water from **wells** and **rivers**, can only carry a small amount at a time. In nature, water crashing onto a beach in a storm is responsible for moving large amounts of **sand** and even **boulders**. There are numerous other examples.

The melting/**freezing point of water** at normal atmospheric pressure is 0° C and the **boiling point** is 100° C. Unusually, the solid form of pure water – ice – is less dense than the liquid – water expands as it freezes. This property explains why icebergs float on the **ocean** and why ice cubes float in a glass of water. The difference in density between liquid water and ice is about one-tenth, so ninetenths of a body of ice is below the water level, with just one-tenth above it.

◀ **Water** – Water is necessary for life. People who are not fortunate enough to have water piped to their homes must carry it, often from far away.

Water

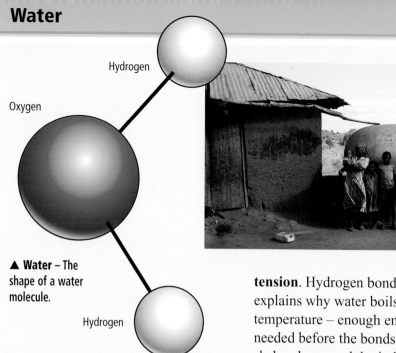

Hydrogen

Oxygen

Hydrogen

▲ **Water** – The shape of a water molecule.

◄ **Water** – Water is a precious resource. Our bodies need water every day to replace what is lost in breathing and sweating. In areas without reliable supplies some people make huge stone jars to collect rain whenever it falls.

Water molecules are shaped like dumb-bells. This gives water another important property: each molecule is positively charged at one end and negatively charged at the other end. Because the molecule is charged, molecules can attract one another (as well as other charged particles). This form of linking is called hydrogen bonding. It explains why water holds together so well.

The same force is also responsible for the strange way in which water behaves when it freezes. Water molecules become locked rigidly together on freezing, but hydrogen bonding ensures that they lock together in a pattern with the hydrogen atoms of one molecule touching the oxygen atoms of its neighbour. This pattern causes the molecules to line up, rather than to pack densely. That is the reason why ice is less dense than liquid water and why snowflakes grow in patterns.

In **ice crystals** the links between molecules are made in a very ordered way, forming patterns. When the water is liquid, the arrangement of molecules is not fixed, but the bonding is still strong, so that water forms drops and clings as films to surfaces and in small spaces – the feature we call **surface tension**. Hydrogen bonding also explains why water boils at a high temperature – enough energy is needed before the bonds can be shaken loose and the individual molecules rise as vapour.

The electrical charge of a water molecule is also important for its ability to dissolve substances. If a substance such as salt (sodium chloride) is placed in water, the charges on the water pull the sodium and the chloride particles apart. The sodium particles (ions) and the chloride particles (ions) then become enclosed in jackets of water molecules, so that they cannot easily join up again unless all of the water is driven off.

Some water molecules even become dragged apart, leaving a few hydrogen (ions) loose in the water. Any substance with free hydrogen ions is an acid, so water can be weakly acidic. This is important in explaining the way that water can dissolve rock in the landscape.

(*For more scientific terms associated with water see:* **Hardness; Head; Heat capacity.**)

(*For types of water see:* **Artesian water; Brackish water; Clean water; Drinking water; Fresh water; Ground water; Polluted water; Sea water.**)

(*See also:* **Water consumption; Water cycle; Water life; Water power; Water resource; Water supply.**)

Water consumption

The amount of **water** that people use, measured in litres per person per day. On average, people throughout the world use about 60 litres per day.

The easier it is to obtain water and the cheaper the water is to buy, the more consumption grows. For those who have to carry water from distant sources by hand, consumption may be as low as 15 litres a day. But when water is easy to obtain, consumption rises dramatically. In the United States, for example, consumption is 380 litres per person per day for home needs. Farming uses far more than this for **irrigation**.

Water consumption changes by day and by season. Consumption is highest in the early morning and later in the day, when people use showers and baths. It may rise when people water their gardens and fill their pools in summer.

Water cycle

The circulation of **water** between the seas, the air, the plants, the rocks and the **rivers**. The energy for this essential cycle comes from the Sun and from gravity. The energy of the Sun allows **evaporation** and powers the winds that carry moist air from the **oceans** to the land, while gravity brings water back from the clouds and rivers to the oceans.

The water cycle – also called the **hydrological cycle** – is the main means of transferring water around the Earth. The main way in which water gets into the air is through **evaporation** from oceans.

The water rises as **vapour** and then changes back into droplets or **ice crystals** high in the air. When **raindrops** or ice crystals reach a large enough size, they can fall out against the rising currents of air and produce **rain** and snow.

Some of the water that reaches the ground is used up in wetting the surfaces of leaves, and to a lesser extent, roads and buildings. This water never reaches the soil but is evaporated back to the air. The remaining water seeps into the soil. Some water is held back by the soil, this time trapped in the tiny cavities between soil grains known as pores. This water will later be sucked up by plant roots and returned as vapour to the air as the plants **transpire**.

Any water not lost by falling on plants or trapped in soils will then drain slowly through the soil and any **permeable rock** as **ground water** before finding its way eventually to the banks and bed of a river. In times of heavy rainfall some water may also run directly over the ground as surface **runoff**, simply because the ground cannot soak it up fast enough.

Rivers return both surface runoff and ground water to the oceans, thus completing the water cycle.

The water cycle can be severely altered by people. The demand for water is now so great that the whole flow of a river is sometimes consumed by people living near its banks. As more and more areas become built up, the amount of impermeable surfaces increases, and less water flows into the ground. This water is taken instead through drains directly to rivers. This makes river flows much more variable. Rivers are more likely to **flood** during heavy **rainfall** and have little water left in times of **drought**.

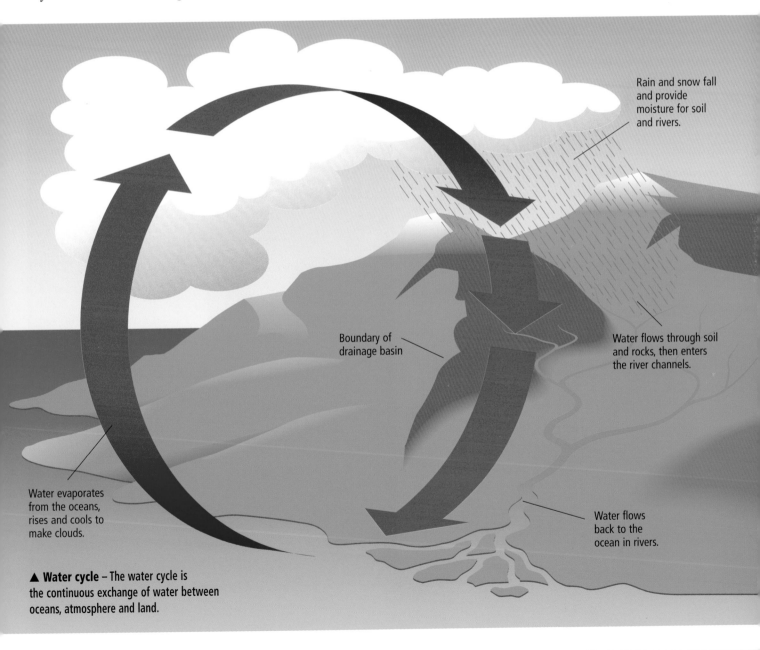

Rain and snow fall and provide moisture for soil and rivers.

Boundary of drainage basin

Water flows through soil and rocks, then enters the river channels.

Water evaporates from the oceans, rises and cools to make clouds.

Water flows back to the ocean in rivers.

▲ **Water cycle** – The water cycle is the continuous exchange of water between oceans, atmosphere and land.

Waterfall

A place where flowing river **water** falls nearly vertically. Waterfalls are sometimes called **cataracts** if the fall contains very large amounts of water (for example, the Nile River cataracts). A waterfall with a small vertical drop, a series of small vertical drops, or a steep slope rather than a drop may be called a cascade. When water is running down a very steep slope, but there are no obvious drops, then the term **rapids** is used. (*See also:* **Fall line**.)

The world's highest waterfall is Angel Falls in Venezuela, with a fall of some 980m. The largest waterfall by volume is the Khone Falls on the Mekong River in Laos, which carries nearly 12,000 cu m of water per second over a fall of 70m.

Waterfalls have many characteristic features. Because the water falls from a great height and contains stones, it can erode the bed at the bottom of the falls. This **erosion** is marked by a deep pool called a plunge pool. If plunge pools grow and the rock forming the fall is undermined, then the waterfall may retreat, its earlier position being marked by a gorge.

Waterfalls by height

Waterfall name	River	Country	Fall in metres
Angel (Churún Merú)	Churún	Venezuela	979
Tugela	Tugela	South Africa	948
Mtarazi	Inyangombe	Zimbabwe	762
Yosemite	Yosemite	United States	739
Cuquenián	Cuquenán	Venezuela	610
Sutherland	Arthur	New Zealand	580
Kile	–	Norway	561
Kahiwa	–	United States	533
Mardal	Eikesdal	Norway	517
Ribbon	Ribbon	United States	491
King George VI	Utshi	Guyana	488
Wollomombi	Wollomombi	Australia	482
Kaliuwaa	Kalanui Stream	United States	463
Kalambo	Kalambo	Tanzania	427
Gavarnie	Gave de Pau	France	422

Waterfalls by volume

Waterfall name	River	Country	Fall in metres	Volume in cu m/s
Khone	Mekong	Kampuchea–Laos	14	11,600
Niagara (Horseshoe)	Niagara	Canada–United States	49	5,525
Paulo Afonso	São Francisco	Brazil	84	2,800
Urubupungá	Paraná	Brazil	12	2,750
Iguaçu	Iguaçu–Paraná	Argentina–Brazil	82	1,750
Victoria	Zambezi	Zambia–Zimbabwe	108	1,080

▼▶ **Waterfall –** Many waterfalls occur where a hard cap rock is found along the course of a river.

River

Waterfall

Overhang

River

Plunge pool

The gorge at Niagara Falls is 11km and, if allowed to flow naturally, would continue to retreat at about the rate of 1m a year.

Waterfalls are mainly new features on the landscape and they do not last long. Older ones gradually erode themselves away, while new ones form. At the moment, because we are still quite close to the end of the last **Ice Age**, the world has more waterfalls than normal, many of them falling down the sides of glacially deepened valleys. Yosemite and Niagara Falls, for example, are both less than 12,000 years old. The world's oldest waterfalls are in Africa and South America. Some of them may be several million years old. Angel Falls, in Venezuela, is one example of an old waterfall. (*See also:* **Fjord**.)

Water life

Water is vital to life. It has a number of special properties that have made it useful to all living things: It is a liquid at normal temperatures; also, it holds heat well (it has a good thermal or **heat capacity**) which means it doesn't change temperature quickly, thus helping minimise changes within, for example, the human body.

No major group of living things originated in **fresh water**. This is because **rivers** and **lakes** are much harsher environments than the **oceans**, where temperatures are very constant. This also means that life in inland waters is much less diverse than in oceans.

In both oceans and fresh water there are three main kinds of life: those that convert the Sun's energy into tissue (the plants); those that use the plants as food (either directly or by eating grazing animals); and those that eat the

bodies of plants and animals once they die (decomposers). In this way the nourishment (nutrients) in the water is recycled for use by new generations.

Estuaries are places where rivers meet the sea. They are where plant nourishment becomes trapped, so they support more life than an equal volume of river or ocean water.

The great mangrove forests of tropical estuaries and estuary marshes of cooler regions depend on this nourishment, as do the free-living plants and the sea grasses that form dense mats on the muddy estuary floor. Plankton also grow rapidly in estuaries because of the amount of trapped nutrients.

The high level of plant matter means that many fish and invertebrates (such as shrimps, clams and crabs) can thrive.

Many estuaries are now important sites for aquaculture (for example, shrimp and salmon farming). However, the same system that traps nourishment can

also trap pollution, and so only estuaries away from settlements can be used for aquaculture. (*See also:* **Ocean life**.)

Water power

Any form of **water** that produces useful energy.

Waterwheels use water power directly, although most water power is now converted into electricity by **hydroelectric power** plants.

Water power is only useful if the flow of water can be kept reasonably steady throughout the year. In many cases the only way to do this is to build **dams** and store water in **reservoirs** behind the dam. The water can then be released steadily from the reservoir. This balances out the natural flow of the **river**, which would otherwise rise after a storm and fall during a **drought**.

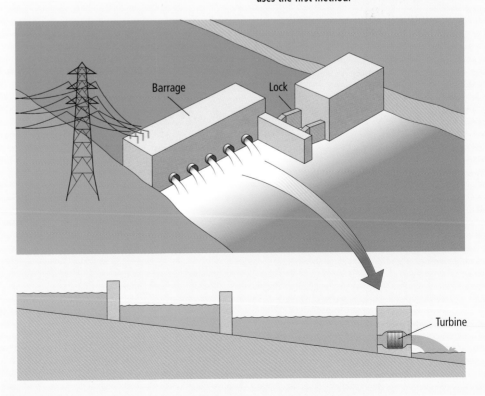

▼ **Water power** – Water power can be produced by either a large volume of water falling from a small height or a smaller volume falling from a large height. This barrage (below) uses the first method.

Barrage   Lock

Turbine

Water resource

Any kind of **water** that is suited to use by people can be thought of as a water resource. The world's water totals 1.4 billion cu km in volume. The largest resource is the oceans, which occupy 71% of the Earth's surface and make up 97.25% by volume of the world's water. Although the oceans are saltwater resources, they can be used to recover their salt content, or through **desalinisation** they can be used to provide **fresh water**. **Sea water** can also be used as cooling water in power plants.

Although fresh water represents a very small part of the total liquid water on Earth, it is a much more useful resource than the oceans because it can be used more easily for **drinking**, for **irrigation** and by industry.

River water can, after purification, be used as a **water supply**. If river valleys are dammed, water can also be stored so that it can be used throughout the year for drinking, industry, irrigation and to generate **hydroelectric power** (*see:* **Dam**). For those who live at some distance from a river, water has to be moved by artificial channel, or **aqueduct**.

Water also seeps into the ground and becomes available in water-bearing rocks called **aquifers**. Many aquifers are recharged in mountainous regions and then carry water underground to lowland areas that have much less reliable **rain**. They are called **artesian** supplies.

Water in the form of **ice** covers Antarctica, Greenland and some of the world's mountains. Ice represents a large amount of **fresh water**, making up 2% of the world's entire water resources. However, it is very difficult to use.

Increasing population means that people need increasingly large

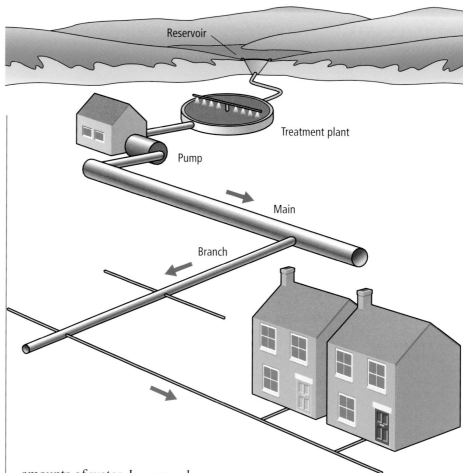

Reservoir

Treatment plant

Pump

Main

Branch

amounts of water. In some places, for example, the southwestern United States, demand and supply are only matched by transferring large amounts of water long distances by aqueduct. The problem of finding enough water is likely to increase in the future.

Water is only a resource for many uses if it is **clean**. Cleaning water is expensive, and polluting water in our rivers only increases the cost of cleaning it. One of the most significant sources of pollution has been the seeping of salt and fertilisers from irrigated soils into aquifers and rivers. Another problem occurs when sewage is not properly dealt with and seeps into river waters.

Watershed

The name used both for the boundary of a **drainage basin**, which divides the **river** basin from its neighbours, and for the whole drainage basin.

▲ **Water supply** – Supplying water requires a reliable, stored reserve, which is distributed via a network of pipes. Giant pumps are used to perform this task.

Water supply

The supply of **water** to people at home and at work. It involves storing water in **reservoirs**, transporting it to centres where it is needed, treating it to make sure it is **clean** and safe for use, and distributing it from the treatment centre to homes, businesses and farms.

We need a water-supply industry because water flows irregularly, it is not always naturally fit to drink, and it only flows in **rivers** and some underground rocks.

A water supply system includes: a source or sources of supply, such as a river or an **aquifer**; some kind of temporary storage, such as a reservoir; a means of transporting water from storage to the treatment plant such as pipes or **aqueducts**; treatment facilities for improving water quality; and more pipes to carry the cleaned water to its consumers. In most cases the used water is then returned to a river after first being cleaned in a treatment plant.

Water supply is extremely important to all countries, and large amounts of money are spent on getting **clean water** to all homes. However, not all countries have enough money for this and many people in the developing world still get their water directly from rivers. As a result, they suffer many more **diseases** than people in wealthy countries. (*See also:* **Desalinisation** and **Irrigation**.)

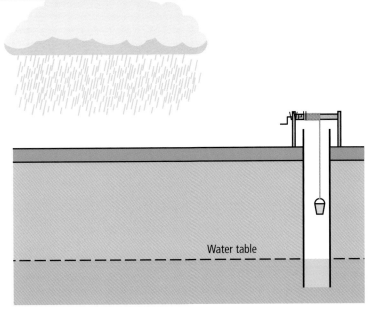

◄ **Well** – A well is sunk to the level of the permanent water table in an underground aquifer.

Water table

Water vapour
(*See:* **Vapour**.)

Well
A vertical shaft that is drilled down into an **aquifer** in order to obtain **water** for **drinking** and other home uses, for industry, or for farming.

A small well, meant to serve a single house, may be about 1m across and lined with brick. The wells needed to supply water to a city are on an altogether different scale. These wells are often sunk many tens of metres down into a large, reliable aquifer. They are not open wells, but enclosed, and are drained by pipes about 30cm across. These wells are sealed so that the **clean water** coming from the well is not contaminated from the surface. The water in these wells is often pumped out of the aquifer with motorised pumps. (*See also:* **Ground water**.)

Water table
The natural level of **water** in a soil or rock. Below the water table the soil or rock is saturated.

When a water table rises to meet the surface of the land, water seeps out of the ground, often as a **spring**. The **head waters** of many **rivers** have formed this way.

The height of a water table is very important for people who rely on **wells** for their water. The water table rises and falls each year, so the depth of water in the **well** also rises and falls. If the well is not deep enough, the falling level in summer can leave the well dry. Some wells need to be over 100m deep to keep them from running dry in summer.

Wetlands
Areas containing shallow **water** or saturated soil, where dead plant matter rots slowly and plants are adapted to wet conditions.

Wetlands include **swamps**, **bogs**, marshes, mires, tundra and fens. They cover about 5% of the land surface of the world.

Rice paddies are artificial wetlands covering about 1 to 2% of the land surface. Half the world's population gets its staple food from these rice paddies.

▼ **Water table** – The water table is the upper surface of waterlogged ground.

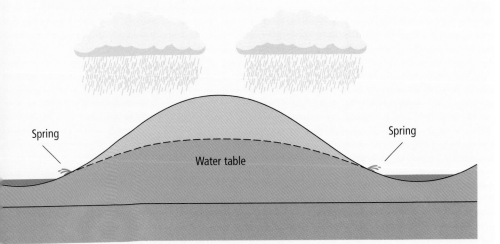

Spring

Spring

Water table

Index